Challenging the Bible

Immediex Publishing

Challenging the Bible

Selections from the Writings and
Speeches of Robert G. Ingersoll

Edited by Dean Tipton

Immediex Publishing

Immediex Publishing
www.immediex.com

Editing / Compilation Copyright © 2005 Dean Tipton

Published in the United States

Printed in the United States

Tipton, Dean

    Challenging the Bible: Selections from the Writings and
Speeches of Robert G. Ingersoll

ISBN 1-932968-26-1

Categories
Religion: General
Religion: Religious Studies
Religion: Christianity

Contents

Introduction   7

From *About the Holy Bible*   9

From *What Would You Substitute for the Bible as a*   59
Moral Guide?

From *The Foundations of Faith*   65

From *The Gods*   73

From *Heretics And Hericies*   91

From *Inspiration Of Bible*   105

From *The Jews*   123

From *Some Mistakes Of Moses*   129

Introduction

The *Bible*! It is the most widely known and read book ever, revered by billions of people throughout the world. It exercises influence—directly or indirectly—on almost every person today, and it has been the most dominant power in human history.

But very few people have challenged the *Bible*.

Can we trust the *Bible* to be the infallible word of God? Is its historical content accurate? Are its teachings valid? Can its instruction be considered moral and righteous? Is it entirely free of internal contradictions?

Sadly, very few people have addressed such issues. And even today, most Biblical criticism neglects fair and broad investigation of the major issues.

But over a century ago, one of the greatest freethinkers and orators of all time—Robert G. Ingersoll—brilliantly, clearly, and thoroughly issued his insights that question the *Bible*.

Robert G. Ingersoll (1833-1899) was a prominent American politician, lecturer, and speaker well known for his Biblical criticism as well as his emphasis on humanism and rationalism.

Ingersoll became a lawyer in his early twenties, and established a prosperous law practice. He then became involved in politics, and also served in the US Civil War in the early 1860s.

Ingersoll later served as Illinois attorney general, as well as a Republican Party spokesman in presidential campaigns, and a figure in various other political roles. He also ran several successful business ventures.

Although Ingersoll was well-connected and financially powerful, he was prevented from high political advancement due to his religious views and his refusal to remain silent about them.

Ingersoll was most well known for his lectures, which became his main focus beginning in the 1870s, and dealt with social, religious, and political issues. They became more outspoken and bold as his speaking career progressed.

A brilliant and dynamic speaker, Ingersoll frequently captivated his audiences and held their attention and interest for several straight hours. His high-demand speeches commanded speaker fees as high as several thousand dollars each—a very large sum in those days. Ingersoll is currently considered by many to be one of the greatest and most powerful orators of all time.

I firmly believe that even today, Ingersoll's material remains among the best on Biblical criticism and analysis. In this book, I have selected and presented some of the best of his thousands and thousands of pages of writings and recorded speeches that challenge the *Bible* and its followers, and I have compiled the material together—all resulting in a truly special work in the genre of religious literature.

Dean Tipton

From *About the Holy Bible*

Somebody ought to tell the truth about the Bible. The preachers dare not, because they would be driven from their pulpits. Professors in colleges dare not, because they would lose their salaries. Politicians dare not. They would be defeated. Editors dare not. They would lose subscribers. Merchants dare not, because they might lose customers. Men of fashion dare not, fearing that they would lose caste. Even clerks dare not, because they might be discharged. And so I thought I would do it myself.

There are many millions of people who believe the Bible to be the inspired word of God—millions who think that this book is staff and guide, counselor and consoler; that it fills the present with peace and the future with hope—millions who believe that it is the fountain of law, Justice and mercy, and that to its wise and benign teachings the world is indebted for its liberty, wealth and civilization—millions who imagine that this book is a revelation from the wisdom and love of God to the brain and heart of man—millions who regard this book as a torch that conquers the darkness of death, and pours its radiance on another world—a world without a tear.

They forget its ignorance and savagery, its hatred of liberty, its religious persecution; they remember heaven, but they forget the dungeon of eternal pain. They forget that it imprisons the brain and corrupts the heart. They forget that it is the enemy of intellectual freedom. Liberty is my religion.

Liberty of hand and brain—of thought and labor, liberty is a word hated by kings—loathed by popes. It is a word that shatters thrones and altars—that leaves the crowned without subjects, and the outstretched hand of superstition without alms. Liberty is the blossom and fruit of justice—the perfume of mercy. Liberty is the seed and soil, the air and light, the dew and rain of progress, love and joy.

THE ORIGIN OF THE BIBLE

A few wandering families... who had been enslaved for four hundred years... had just escaped from their masters to the desert of Sinai. Their leader was Moses, a man who had been raised in the family of Pharaoh and had been taught the law and mythology of Egypt. For the purpose of controlling his followers he pretended that he was instructed and assisted by Jehovah, the God of these wanderers.

Everything that happened was attributed to the interference of this God. Moses declared that he met this God face to face; that on Sinai's top from the hands of this God he had received the tables of stone on which, by the finger of this God, the Ten Commandments had been written, and that, in addition to this, Jehovah had made known the sacrifices and ceremonies that were pleasing to him and the laws by which the people should be governed.

In this way the Jewish religion and the Mosaic Code were established.

It is now claimed that this religion and these laws were and are revealed and established for all mankind.

At that time these wanderers had no commerce with other nations, they had no written language, they could neither read nor write. They had no means by which they could make this revelation known to other nations, and so it remained buried in the jargon of a few... impoverished and unknown tribes for more than two thousand years.

Many centuries after Moses, the leader, was dead many centuries after all his followers had passed away—the Pentateuch was written, the work of many writers, and to give it force and authority it was claimed that Moses was the author.

We now know that the Pentateuch was not written by Moses. Towns are mentioned that were not in existence when Moses lived. ...

So many of the laws were not applicable to wanderers on the desert—laws about agriculture, about the sacrifice of oxen, sheep and doves, about the weaving of cloth, about ornaments of gold and silver, about the cultivation of land, about harvest, about the threshing of grain, about houses and temples, about cities of refuge, and about many other subjects of no possible application to a few starving wanderers over the sands and rocks.

It is now not only admitted by intelligent and honest theologians that Moses was not the author of the Pentateuch, but they all admit that no one knows who the authors were, or who wrote any one of these books, or a chapter or a line. We know that the books were not written in the same generation; that they were not all written by one person; that they are filled with mistakes and contradictions. It is also admitted that Joshua did not write the book that bears his name, because it refers to events that did not happen until long after his death.

No one knows, or pretends to know, the author of Judges; all we know is that it was written centuries after all the judges had ceased to exist. No one knows the author of Ruth, nor of First and Second Samuel; all we know is that Samuel did not write the books that bear his name. In the 25th chapter of First Samuel is an account of the raising of Samuel by the Witch of Endor.

No one knows the author of First and Second Kings or First and Second Chronicles; all we know is that these books are of no value.

We know that the Psalms were not written by David. In the Psalms the Captivity is spoken of, and that did not happen until about five hundred years after David slept with his fathers.

We know that Solomon did not write the Proverbs or the Song; that Isaiah was not the author of the book that bears his name; that no one knows the author of Job, Ecclesiastes, or Esther, or of any book in the Old Testament, with the exception of Ezra.

We know that God is not mentioned or in any way referred to in the book of Esther. We know, too, that the book is cruel, absurd and impossible.

God is not mentioned in the Song of Solomon, the best book in the Old Testament.

And we know that Ecclesiastes was written by an unbeliever.

We know, too, that the Jews themselves had not decided as to what books were inspired—were authentic—until the second century after Christ.

We know that the idea of inspiration was of slow growth, and that the inspiration was determined by those who had certain ends to accomplish.

IS THE OLD TESTAMENT INSPIRED?

If it is, it should be a book that no man—no number of men—could produce. It should contain the perfection of philosophy. It should perfectly accord with every fact in nature. There should be no mistakes in astronomy, geology, or as to any subject or science. Its morality should be the highest, the purest. Its laws and regulations for the control of conduct should be just, wise, perfect, and perfectly adapted to the accomplishment of the ends desired. It should contain nothing calculated to make man cruel, revengeful, vindictive or infamous. It should be filled with intelligence, justice, purity, honesty, mercy and the spirit of liberty. It should be opposed to strife and war, to slavery and lust, to ignorance, credulity and superstition. It should develop the brain and civilize the heart. It should satisfy the heart and brain of the best and wisest. It should be true.

Does the Old Testament satisfy this standard? Is there anything in the Old Testament—in history, in theory, in law, in government, in morality, in science—above and beyond the ideas, the beliefs, the customs and prejudices of its authors and the people among whom they lived? Is there one ray of light from any supernatural source?

The ancient Hebrews believed that this earth was the center of the universe, and that the sun, moon and stars were specks in the sky. With this the Bible agrees.

They thought the earth was flat, with four corners; that the sky, the firmament, was solid—the floor of Jehovah's house. The Bible teaches the same.

They imagined that the sun journeyed about the earth, and that by stopping the sun the day could be lengthened. The Bible agrees with this.

They believed that Adam and Eve were the first man and woman; that they had been created but a few years before, and that they, the Hebrews, were their direct descendants. This the Bible teaches.

If anything is, or can be, certain, the writers of the Bible were mistaken about creation, astronomy, geology; about the causes of phenomena, the origin of evil and the cause of death.

Now, it must be admitted that if an infinite Being is the author of the Bible, he knew all sciences, all facts, and could not have made a mistake.

If, then, there are mistakes, misconceptions, false

theories, ignorant myths and blunders in the Bible, it must have been written by finite beings; that is to say, by ignorant and mistaken men.

Nothing can be clearer than this.

For centuries the church insisted that the Bible was absolutely true; that it contained no mistakes; that the story of creation was true; that its astronomy and geology were in accord with the facts; that the scientists who differed with the Old Testament were infidels and atheists.

Now this has changed. The educated Christians admit that the writers of the Bible were not inspired as to any science. They now say that God, or Jehovah, did not inspire the writers of his book for the purpose of instructing the world about astronomy, geology, or any science. They now admit that the inspired men who wrote the Old Testament knew nothing about any science, and that they wrote about the earth and stars, the sun and moon, in accordance with the general ignorance of the time.

It required many centuries to force the theologians to this admission. Reluctantly, full of malice and hatred, the priests retired from the field, leaving the victory with science.

They took another position; They declared that the authors, or rather the writers, of the Bible were inspired in spiritual and moral things; that Jehovah wanted to make known to his children his will and his infinite love for his children; that Jehovah, seeing his people wicked, ignorant and depraved, wished to make them merciful and just, wise and spiritual, and that the Bible is inspired in its laws, in the religion it teaches and in its ideas of government.

This is the issue now. Is the Bible any nearer right in its ideas of justice, of mercy, of morality or of religion than in its conception of the sciences? Is it moral?

It upholds slavery... Could a devil have done worse?

Is it merciful? In war it raised the black flag; it commanded the destruction, the massacre, of all—of the old, infirm, and helpless—of wives and babes.

Were its laws inspired? Hundreds of offenses were punished with death. To pick up sticks on Sunday, to murder your father on Monday, were equal crimes. There is in the literature of the world no bloodier code. The law of revenge—of retaliation—was the law of Jehovah. An eye for an eye, a tooth for a tooth, a limb for a limb. This is savagery—not philosophy.

Is it just and reasonable? The Bible is opposed to religious toleration—to religious liberty. Whoever differed with the majority was stoned to death. Investigation was a crime. Husbands were ordered to denounce and to assist in killing their unbelieving wives.

It is the enemy of Art. "Thou shalt make no graven image." This was the death of Art. Palestine never produced a painter or a sculptor.

Is the Bible civilized? It upholds lying, larceny, robbery, murder, the selling of diseased meat to strangers, and even the sacrifice of human beings to Jehovah.

Is it philosophical? It teaches that the sins of a people can be transferred to an animal—to a goat. It makes maternity an offence for which a sin offering had to be made. It was wicked to give birth to a boy, and twice as wicked to give birth to a girl. To make hair-oil like that used by the priests was an offence punishable with death. The blood of a bird killed over running water was regarded as medicine.

Would a civilized God daub his altars with the blood of oxen, lambs and doves? Would he make all his priests butchers? Would he delight in the smell of burning flesh?

THE TEN COMMANDMENTS

Some Christian lawyers—some eminent and stupid judges—have said and still say, that the Ten Commandments are the foundation of all law.

Nothing could be more absurd. Long before these commandments were given there were codes of laws in India and Egypt—laws against murder, perjury, larceny, adultery and fraud. Such laws are as old as human society; as old as the love of life; as old as industry; as the idea of prosperity; as old as human love.

All of the Ten Commandments that are good were old; all that were new are foolish. If Jehovah had been civilized he would have left out the commandment about keeping the Sabbath, and in its place would have said: "Thou shalt not enslave thy fellow-men." ... He would have left out the one about graven images, and in its stead would have said: "Thou shalt not wage wars of extermination, and thou shalt not unsheathe the sword except in self-defence."

If Jehovah had been civilized, how much grander the Ten Commandments would have been.

All that we call progress—the enfranchisement of man, of labor, the substitution of imprisonment for death, of fine for imprisonment, the destruction of polygamy, the establishing of free speech, of the rights of conscience; in short, all that has tended to the development and civilization of man; all the results of investigation, observation, experience and free thought; all that man has accomplished for the benefit of man since the close of the Dark Ages—has been done in spite of the Old Testament.

Let me further illustrate the morality, the mercy, the philosophy and goodness of the Old Testament:

The Story of Achan

Joshua took the City of Jericho. Before the fall of the city he declared that all the spoil taken should be given to the Lord.

In spite of this order Achan secreted a garment, some silver and gold.

Afterward Joshua tried to take the city of Ai. He failed and many of his soldiers were slain. Joshua sought for the cause of his defeat and he found that Achan had secreted a garment, two hundred shekels of silver and a wedge of gold. To this Achan confessed.

And thereupon Joshua took Achan, his sons and his

daughters, his oxen and his sheep—stoned them all to death and burned their bodies.

There is nothing to show that the sons and daughters had committed any crime. Certainly, the oxen and sheep should not have been stoned to death for the crime of their owner. This was the justice, the mercy, of Jehovah!

After Joshua had committed this crime, with the help of Jehovah he captured the city of Ai.

The Story of Elisha

"And he went up thence unto Bethel, and as he was going up by the way there came forth little children out of the city and mocked him, and said unto him, 'Go up, thou baldhead.'

"And he turned back and looked at them, and cursed them in the name of the Lord. And there came forth two she-bears out of the wood and tore forty and two children of them."

This was the work of the good God—the merciful Jehovah!

The Story of Daniel

King Darius had honored and exalted Daniel, and the native princes were jealous. So they induced the king to sign a decree to the effect that any man who should make a petition to any god or man except to King Darius, for thirty days, should be cast into the den of lions.

Afterward these men found that Daniel, with his face toward Jerusalem, prayed three times a day to Jehovah. Thereupon Daniel was cast into the den of lions; a stone was placed at the mouth of the den and sealed with the king's seal.

The king passed a bad night. The next morning he went to the den and cried out to Daniel. Daniel answered and told the king that God had sent his angel and shut the mouths of the lions.

Daniel was taken out alive and well, and the king was converted and believed in Daniel's God.

Darius, being then a believer in the true God, sent for the men who had accused Daniel, and for their wives and their children, and cast them all into the lions' den.

"And the lions had the mastery of them, and brake all their bones in pieces, or ever they came at the bottom of the pit."

What had the wives and little children done? How had they offended King Darius, the believer in Jehovah? Who protected Daniel? Jehovah! Who failed to protect the innocent wives and children? Jehovah!

WHAT IS IT ALL WORTH?

Will some Christian scholar tell us the value of Genesis?

We know that it is not true—that it contradicts itself. There are two accounts of the creation in the first and second chapters. In the first account birds and beasts were created before man. In the second, man was created before the birds and beasts.

In the first, fowls are made out of the water. In the second, fowls are made out of the ground.

In the first, Adam and Eve are created together. In the second, Adam is made; then the beasts and birds, and then Eve is created from one of Adam's ribs. ...

... [In all of Genesis,] Is there an elevated thought—any great principle—anything poetic—any word that bursts into blossom?

Is there anything except a dreary and detailed statement of things that never happened?

Is there anything in Exodus calculated to make men generous, loving and noble?

Is it well to teach children that God tortured the innocent cattle of the Egyptians—bruised them to death with hailstones—on account of the sins of Pharaoh?

Does it make us merciful to believe that God killed the firstborn of the Egyptians—the firstborn of the poor and suffering people—of the poor girl working at the mill—because of the wickedness of the king?

Can we believe that the gods of Egypt worked miracles? Did they change water into blood, and sticks into serpents?

In Exodus there is not one original thought or line of value. We know, if we know anything, that this book was written by savages—savages who believed in slavery, polygamy and wars of extermination. We know that the story told is impossible, and that the miracles were never performed. This book admits that there are other gods besides Jehovah. In the 17th chapter is this verse: "Now I know that the Lord is greater than all gods, for, in the thing wherein they dealt proudly, he was above them."

So, in this blessed book is taught the duty of human sacrifice—the sacrifice of babes.

In the 22nd chapter is this command: "Thou shalt not delay to offer the first of thy ripe fruits and of thy liquors: the firstborn of thy sons thou shalt give unto me."

Has Exodus been a help or a hindrance to the human race?

Take from Exodus the laws common to all nations, and is there anything of value left?

Is there anything in Leviticus of importance? Is there a chapter worth reading? What interest have we in the clothes of priests, the curtains and candles of the tabernacle, the tongs and shovels of the altar or the hair-oil used by the Levities?

Of what use the cruel code, the frightful punishments, the curses, the falsehoods and the miracles of this ignorant and infamous book?

And what is there in the book of Numbers—with its sacrifices and water of jealousy, with its shewbread and spoons, its kids and fine flour, its oil and candlesticks, its cucumbers, onions and manna—to assist and instruct mankind? What interest have we in the rebellion of Korah, the water of separation, the ashes of a red heifer, the brazen serpent, the water that followed the people uphill and down for forty years, and the inspired donkey of the prophet

Balaam?   Have these absurdities and cruelties—these childish, savage superstitions—helped to civilize the world?

Is there anything in Joshua—with its wars, its murders and massacres, its swords dripping with the blood of mothers and babes, its tortures, maimings and mutilations, its fraud and fury, its hatred and revenge—calculated to improve the world?

Does not every chapter shock the heart of a good man? Is it a book to be read by children?

The book of Joshua is as merciless as famine, as ferocious as the heart of a wild beast. It is a history—a justification—a sanctification of nearly every crime.

The book of Judges is about the same, nothing but war and bloodshed; the horrible story of Jael and Sisera; of Gideon and his trumpets and pitchers; of Jephtha and his daughter, whom he murdered to please Jehovah.

Here we find the story of Samson, in which a sun-god is changed to a Hebrew giant.

Read this book of Joshua—read of the slaughter of women, of wives, of mothers and babes—read its impossible miracles, its ruthless crimes, and all done according to the commands of Jehovah, and tell me whether this book is calculated to make us forgiving, generous and loving.

I admit that the history of Ruth is in some respects a beautiful and touching story; that it is naturally told, and that her love for Naomi was deep and pure. But in the matter of courtship we would hardly advise our daughters to follow the example of Ruth. Still, we must remember that Ruth was a widow.

Is there anything worth reading in the first and second books of Samuel? Ought a prophet of God to hew a captured king in pieces? Is the story of the ark, its capture and return of importance to us? Is it possible that it was right, just and merciful to kill fifty thousand men because they had looked into a box? Of what use to us are the wars of Saul and David, the stories of Goliath and the Witch of Endor? Why should Jehovah have killed Uzzah for putting forth his hand to steady the ark, and forgiven David for murdering Uriah and stealing his wife?

According to "Samuel," David took a census of the people. This excited the wrath of Jehovah, and as a punishment he allowed David to choose seven years of famine, a flight of three months from pursuing enemies, or three days of pestilence. David, having confidence in God, chose the three days of pestilence; and. thereupon, God, the compassionate, on account of the sin of David, killed seventy thousand innocent men.

Under the same circumstances, what would a devil have done?

Is there anything in first and Second Kings that suggests the idea of inspiration?

When David is dying he tells his son Solomon to murder Joab—not to let his hoar head go down to the grave in peace. With his last breath he commands his son to bring down the hoar head of Shimei to the grave with blood. Having uttered these merciful words, the good David, the man after God's heart, slept with his fathers.

Was it necessary to inspire the man who wrote the history of the building of the temple, the story of the visit of the Queen of Sheba, or to tell the number of Solomon's wives?

What care we for the withering of Jeroboam's hand, the prophecy of Jehu, or the story of Elijah and the ravens?

Can we believe that Elijah brought flames from heaven, or that he went at last to Paradise in a chariot of fire?

Can we believe in the multiplication of the widow's oil by Elisha, that an army was smitten with blindness, or that an axe floated in the water?

Does it civilize us to read about the beheading of the seventy sons of Ahab, the putting out of the eyes of Zedekiah and the murder of his sons? Is there one word in First and Second Kings calculated to make men better?

First and Second Chronicles is but a retelling of what is told in First and Second Kings. The same old stories—a little left out, a little added, but in no respect made better or worse.

The book of Ezra is of no importance. He tells us that Cyrus, King of Persia, issued a proclamation for building a temple at Jerusalem, and that he declared Jehovah to be the real and only God.

Nothing could be more absurd. Ezra tells us about the return from captivity, the building of the Temple, the dedication, a few prayers, and this is all. This book is of no importance, of no use.

Nehemiah is about the same, only it tells of the building of the wall, the complaints of the people about taxes, a list of those who returned from Babylon, a catalogue of those who dwelt at Jerusalem, and the dedication of the walls. Not a word in Nehemiah worth reading.

Then comes the book of Esther: In this we are told that King Ahasueras was intoxicated; that he sent for his Queen, Vashti, to come and show herself to him and his guests. Vashti refused to appear. This maddened the king, and he ordered that from every province the most beautiful girls should be brought before him that he might choose one in place of Vashti. Among others was brought Esther, a Jewess. She was chosen and became the wife of the king. Then a gentleman by the name of Haman wanted to have all the Jews killed, and the king, not knowing that Esther was of that race, signed a decree that all the Jews should be killed. Through the efforts of Mordecai and Esther the decree was annulled and the Jews were saved. Haman prepared a gallows on which to have Mordecai hanged, but the good Esther so managed matters that Haman and his ten sons were hanged on the gallows that Haman had built, and the Jews were allowed to murder more than seventy-five thousand of the king's subjects. This is the inspired story of Esther.

In the book of Job we find some elevated sentiments, some sublime and foolish thoughts, something of the wonder and sublimity of nature, the joys and sorrows of life; but the story is infamous.

Some of the Psalms are good, many are indifferent, a few are infamous. In them are mingled the vices and virtues. There are verses that elevate, verses that degrade. There are prayers for forgiveness and revenge. In the literature of the world there is nothing more heartless, more infamous, than the 109th Psalm. ←?

In the Proverbs there is much shrewdness, many pithy and prudent maxims, many wise sayings. The same ideas are expressed in many ways—the wisdom of economy and silence, the dangers of vanity and idleness. Some are trivial, some are foolish, and many are wise. These proverbs are not generous—not altruistic. Sayings to the same effect are found among all nations.

Ecclesiastes is the most thoughtful book in the Bible. It was written by an unbeliever—a philosopher—an agnostic. Take out the interpolations, and it is in accordance with the thought of the nineteenth century. In this book are found the most philosophic and poetic passages in the Bible.

After crossing the desert of death and crime, after reading the Pentateuch, Joshua, Judges, Samuel, Kings and Chronicles—it is delightful to reach this grove of palms, called the "Song of Solomon." A drama of love—of human low; a poem without Jehovah—a poem born of the heart and true to the divine instincts of the soul.

"I sleep, but my heart waketh."

Isaiah is the work of several. Its swollen words, its vague imagery, its prophecies and curses, its ravings against kings and nations, its laughter at the wisdom of man, its hatred of joy, have not the slightest tendency to increase the well-being of man.

In this book is recorded the absurdist of all miracles. The

shadow on the dial is turned back ten degrees, in order to satisfy Hezekiah that Jehovah will add fifteen years to his life.

In this miracle the world, turning from west to east at the rate of more than a thousand miles an hour, is not only stopped, but made to turn the other way until the shadow on the dial went back ten degrees! Is there in the whole world an intelligent man or woman who believes this impossible falsehood?

Jeremiah contains nothing of importance—no facts of value; nothing but fault-finding, lamentations, croakings, wailings, curses and promises; nothing but famine and prayer, the prosperity of the wicked, the ruin of the Jews, the captivity and return, and at last Jeremiah, the traitor, in the stocks and in prison.

And Lamentations is simply a continuance of the ravings of the same insane pessimist; nothing but dust and sackcloth and ashes, tears and howls, railings and revilings.

And Ezekiel—eating manuscripts, prophesying siege and desolation, with visions of coals of fire, and cherubim, and wheels with eyes, and the type and figure of the boiling pot, and the resurrection of dry bones—is of no use, of no possible value.

With Voltaire, I say that any one who admires Ezekiel should be compelled to dine with him.

Daniel is a disordered dream—a nightmare. What can be made of this book with its image with a golden head, with breast and arms of silver, with belly and thighs of brass, with legs of iron, and with feet of iron and clay; with its writing on the wall, its den of lions, and its vision of the ram and goat?

Is there anything to be learned from Hosea and his wife? Is there anything of use in Joel, in Amos, in Obadiah? Can we get any good from Jonah and his gourd? Is it possible that God is the real author of Micah and Nahum, of Habakkuk and Zephaniah, of Haggai and Malachi and Zechariah, with his red horses, his four horns, his four carpenters, his flying roll, his mountains of brass and the stone with four eyes?

Is there anything in these "inspired" books that has been of benefit to man? Have they taught us how to cultivate the earth, to build houses, to weave cloth, to prepare food? Have they taught us to paint pictures, to chisel statues, to build bridges, or ships, or anything of beauty or of use? Did we get our ideas of government, of religious freedom, of the liberty of thought, from the Old Testament? Did we get from any of these books a hint of any science? Is there in the "sacred volume" a word, a line, that has added to the wealth, the intelligence and the happiness of mankind? Is there one of the books of the Old Testament as entertaining as "Robinson Crusoe," "The Travels of Gulliver," or "Peter Wilkins and his Flying Wife"? Did the author of Genesis know as much about nature as Humboldt, or Darwin, or Haeckel? Is what is called the Mosaic Code as wise or as merciful as the code of any civilized nation? Were the writers of Kings and Chronicles as great historians, as great writers, as Gibbon and Draper? Is Jeremiah or Habakkuk equal to Dickens or Thackeray? Can the authors of Job and the Psalms be compared with Shakespeare? Why should we attribute the best to man and the worst to God?

WAS JEHOVAH A GOD OF LOVE?

Did these words come from the heart of love?—"When the Lord thy God shall drive them before thee, thou shalt smite them and utterly destroy them; thou shalt make no covenant with them, or show mercy unto them."

"I will heap mischief upon them. I will send mine arrows upon them; they shall be burned with hunger and devoured with burning heat and with bitter destruction."

"I will send the tooth of beasts upon them, with the poison of serpents of the dust."

"The sword without, and terror within, shall destroy both the young man and the virgin; the suckling also with the man of gray hairs."

"Let his children be fatherless and his wife a widow; let his children be continually vagabonds and beg; let them seek their bread also out of their desolate places; let the extortioner catch all that he hath, and let the stranger spoil his labor; let there be none to extend mercy unto him, neither let there be any to favor his fatherless children."

"And thou shalt eat the fruit of thine own body—the flesh of thy sons and daughters."

"And the heaven that is over thee shall be brass, and the earth that is under thee shall be iron."

"Cursed shalt thou be in the city, and cursed shalt thou be

in the field."

"I will make my arrows drunk with blood."

"I will laugh at their calamity."

Did these curses, these threats, come from the heart of love or from the mouth of savagery?

Was Jehovah god or devil?   Why should we place Jehovah above all the gods?

Has man in his ignorance and fear ever imagined a greater monster?   Have the barbarians of any land, in any time, worshiped a more heartless god?

Brahma was a thousand times nobler, and so was Osiris and Zeus and Jupiter.   So was the supreme god of the Aztecs, to whom they offered only the perfume of flowers.   The worst god of the Hindus, with his necklace of skulls and his bracelets of living snakes, was kind and merciful compared with Jehovah.

Compared with Marcus Aurelius, how small Jehovah seems.   Compared with Abraham Lincoln, how cruel, how contemptible, is this god.

JEHOVAH'S ADMINISTRATION

He created the world, the hosts of heaven, a man and woman—placed them in a garden.   Then the serpent deceived them, and they were cast out and made to earn their bread. Jehovah had been thwarted.

Then he tried again.   He went on for about sixteen

hundred years trying to civilize the people.

No schools, no churches, no Bible, no tracts—nobody taught to read or write. No Ten Commandments. The people grew worse and worse, until the merciful Jehovah sent the flood and drowned all the people except Noah and his family, eight in all.

Then he started again, and changed their diet. At first Adam and Eve were vegetarians. After the flood Jehovah said: "Every moving thing that liveth shall be meat for you"— snakes and buzzards.

Then he failed again, and at the Tower of Babel he dispersed and scattered the people.

Finding that he could not succeed with all the people, he thought he would try a few, so he selected Abraham and his descendants. Again he failed, and his chosen people were captured by the Egyptians and enslaved for four hundred years.

Then he tried again—rescued them from Pharaoh and started for Palestine.

Then he changed their diet, allowing them to eat only the beasts that parted the hoof and chewed the cud. Again he failed. The people hated him, and preferred the slavery of Egypt to the freedom of Jehovah. So he kept them wandering until nearly all who came from Egypt had died. Then he tried again—took them into Palestine and had them governed by Judges.

This, too, was a failure—no schools, no Bible. Then he tried kings, and the kings were mostly idolaters.

Then the chosen people were conquered and carried into captivity by the Babylonians.

Another failure.

Then they returned, and Jehovah tried prophets—howlers and wailers—but the people grew worse and worse. No schools, no sciences, no arts, no commerce.

Then Jehovah took upon himself flesh, was born of a woman, and lived among the people that he had been trying to civilize for several thousand years. Then these people, following the law that Jehovah had given them in the wilderness, charged this Jehovah-man—this Christ—with blasphemy; tried, convicted and killed him.

Jehovah had failed again.

Then he deserted the Jews and turned his attention to the rest of the world.

And now the Jews, deserted by Jehovah, persecuted by Christians, are the most prosperous people on the earth. Again has Jehovah failed.

What an administration!

THE NEW TESTAMENT

Who wrote the New Testament?

Christian scholars admit that they do not know. They admit that, if the four gospels were written by Matthew, Mark, Luke and John, they must have been written in Hebrew. And yet a Hebrew manuscript of any one of these gospels has never been found.   All have been and are in Greek.   So, educated theologians admit that the Epistles, James and Jude, were written by persons who had never seen one of the four gospels. In these Epistles—in James and Jude—no reference is made to any of the gospels, nor to any miracle recorded in them.

The first mention that has been found of one of our gospels was made about one hundred and eight years after the birth of Christ, and the four gospels were first named and quoted from at the beginning of the third century, about one hundred an seventy years after the death of Christ.

We now know that there were many other gospels besides our four, some of which have been lost. There were the gospels of Paul, of the Egyptians, of the Hebrews, of Perfection, of Judas, of Thaddeus, of the Infancy, of Thomas, of Mary, of Andrew, of Nicodemus, of Marcion and several others.

So there were the Acts of Pilate, of Andrew, of Mary, of Paul and Thecla and of many others; also a book called the Shepherd of Hermas.

At first not one of all the books was considered as inspired. The Old Testament was regarded as divine; but the books that now constitute the New Testament were regarded as human productions. We now know that we do not know who wrote the four gospels.

The question is, Were the authors of these four gospels inspired?

If they were inspired, then the four gospels mast be true.

If they are true, they mast agree.

The four gospels do not agree.

Matthew, Mark and Luke knew nothing of the atonement, nothing of salvation by faith. They knew only the gospel of good deeds—of charity. They teach that if we forgive others God will forgive us.

With this the gospel of John does not agree.

In that gospel we are taught that we must believe on the Lord Jesus Christ; that we must be born again; that we must drink the blood and eat the flesh of Christ. In this gospel we find the doctrine of the atonement and that Christ died for us and suffered in our place.

This gospel is utterly at variance with the other three. If the other three are true, the gospel of John is false. If the gospel of John was written by an inspired man, the writers of the other three were uninspired. From this there is no possible escape. The four cannot be true.

It is evident that there are many interpolations in the four gospels.

For instance, in the 28th chapter of Matthew is an account to the effect that the soldiers at the tomb of Christ were bribed to say that the disciples of Jesus stole away his body while they, the soldiers, slept.

This is clearly an interpolation. It is a break in the narrative.

The 10th verse should be followed by the 16th. The 10th verse is as follows:

"Then Jesus said unto them, 'Be not afraid; go tell my

brethren that they go unto Galilee and there shall they see me.'"

The 16th verse:

"Then the eleven disciples went away unto Galilee into a mountain, where Jesus had appointed them."

The story about the soldiers contained in the 11th, 12th, 13th, 14th and 15th verses is an interpolation—an afterthought—long after. The 15th verse demonstrates this.

Fifteenth verse: "So they took the money and did as they were taught. And this saying is commonly reported among the Jews until this day."

Certainly this account was not in the original gospel, and certainly the 15th verse was not written by a Jew. No Jew could have written this: "And this saying is commonly reported among the Jews until this day."

Mark, John and Luke never heard that the soldiers had been bribed by the priests; or, if they had, did not think it worth while recording. So the accounts of the Ascension of Jesus Christ in Mark and Luke are interpolations. Matthew says nothing about the Ascension.

Certainly there never was a greater miracle, and yet Matthew, who was present—who saw the Lord rise, ascend and disappear—did not think it worth mentioning.

On the other hand, the last words of Christ, according to Matthew, contradict the Ascension: "Lo I am with you always, even unto the end of the world."

John, who was present, if Christ really ascended, says not one word on the subject.

As to the Ascension, the gospels do not agree.

Mark gives the last conversation that Christ had with his disciples, as follows:

"Go ye into all the world and preach the gospel to every creature. He that believeth and is baptized shall be saved; but he that believeth not shall be damned. And these signs shall follow them that believe: In my name shall they cast out devils; they shall speak with new tongues. They shall take up serpents, and if they drink any deadly thing it shall not hurt them; they shall lay hands on the sick and they shall recover. So, then, after the Lord had spoken unto them, he was received up into heaven and sat on the right hand of God."

Is it possible that this description was written by one who witnessed this miracle?

This miracle is described by Luke as follows.

"And it came to pass while he blessed them he was parted from them and carried up into heaven."

"Brevity is the soul of wit."

In the Acts we are told that: "When he had spoken, while they beheld, he was taken up, and a cloud received him out of their sight."

Neither Luke, nor Matthew, nor John, nor the writer of the Acts, heard one word of the conversation attributed to Christ by Mark. The fact is that the Ascension of Christ was not claimed by his disciples.

At first Christ was a man—nothing more. Mary was his mother, Joseph his father. The genealogy of his father, Joseph, was given to show that he was of the blood of David.

Then the claim was made that he was the son of God, and that his mother was a virgin, and that she remained a virgin until her death.

Then the claim was made that Christ rose from the dead and ascended bodily to heaven.

It required many years for these absurdities to take possession of the minds of men.

If Christ rose from the dead, why did he not appear to his enemies? Why did he not call on Caiaphas, the high priest? Why did he not make another triumphal entry into Jerusalem?

If he really ascended, why did he not do so in public, in the presence of his persecutors? Why should this, the greatest of miracles, be done in secret in a corner?

It was a miracle that could have been seen by a vast multitude—a miracle that could not be simulated—one that would have convinced hundreds of thousands.

After the story of the Resurrection, the Ascension became a necessity. They had to dispose of the body.

So there are many other interpolations in the gospels and epistles.

Again I ask: Is the New Testament true? Does anybody now believe that at the birth of Christ there was a celestial greeting; that a star led the Wise Men of the East; that Herod slew the babes of Bethlehem of two years old and under?

The gospels are filled with accounts of miracles. Were they ever performed?

Matthew gives the particulars of about twenty-two miracles, Mark of about nineteen, Luke of about eighteen and

John of about seven.

According to the gospels, Christ healed diseases, cast out devils, rebuked the sea, cured the blind, fed multitudes with five loaves and two fishes, walked on the sea, cursed a fig tree, turned water into wine and raised the dead.

Matthew is the only one that tells about the Star and the Wise Men—the only one that tells about the murder of babes.

John is the only one who says anything about the resurrection of Lazarus, and Luke is the only one giving an account of the rising from the dead the widow of Nain's son.

How is it possible to substantiate these miracles?

The Jews, among whom they were said to have been performed, did not believe them. The diseased, the palsied, the leprous, the blind who were cured, did not become followers of Christ. Those that were raised from the dead were never heard of again.

Does any intelligent man believe in the existence of devils? The writer of three of the gospels certainly did. John says nothing about Christ having cast out devils, but Matthew, Mark and Luke give many instances.

Does any natural man now believe that Christ cast out devils? If his disciples said he did, they were mistaken. If Christ said he did, he was insane or an impostor.

If the accounts of casting out devils are false, then the writers were ignorant or dishonest. If they wrote through ignorance, then they were not inspired. If they wrote what they knew to be false, they were not inspired. If what they wrote is untrue, whether they knew it or not, they were not inspired.

At that time it was believed that palsy, epilepsy, deafness, insanity and many other diseases were caused by devils; that devils took possession of and lived in the bodies of men and women. Christ believed this, taught this belief to others, and pretended to cure diseases by casting devils out of the sick and insane. ...

Is it a fact that the Devil tried to bribe Christ? Is it a fact that the Devil carried Christ to the top of the temple and tried to induce him to leap to the ground? How can these miracles be established?

The principals have written nothing, Christ has written nothing, and the Devil has remained silent.

How can we know that the Devil tried to bribe Christ? Who wrote the account? We do not know. How did the writer get his information? We do not know.

Somebody, some seventeen hundred years ago, said that the Devil tried to bribe God; that the Devil carried God to the top of the temple and tried to induce him to leap to the earth and that God was intellectually too keen for the Devil.

This is all the evidence we have.

Is there anything in the literature, of the world more perfectly idiotic?

Intelligent people no longer believe in witches, wizards, spooks and devils, and they are perfectly satisfied that every word in the New Testament about casting out devils is utterly false.

Can we believe that Christ raised the dead?

A widow living in Nain is following the body of her son to the tomb. Christ halts the funeral procession and raises the young man from the dead and gives him back to the arms of his mother.

This young man disappears. He is never heard of again. No one takes the slightest interest in the man who returned from the realm of death. Luke is the only one who tells the story. Maybe Matthew, Mark and John never heard of it, or did not believe it and so failed to record it.

John says that Lazarus was raised from the dead; Matthew, Mark and Luke say nothing about it.

It was more wonderful than the raising of the widow's son. He had not been laid in the tomb for days. He was only on his way to the grave, but Lazarus was actually dead. He had begun to decay.

Lazarus did not excite the least interest. No one asked him about the other world. No one inquired of him about their dead friends. When he died the second time no one said: "He is not afraid. He has traveled that road twice and knows just where he is going."

We do not believe in the miracles of Mohammed, and yet they are as well attested as this. We have no confidence in the miracles performed by Joseph Smith, and yet the evidence is far greater, far better.

If a man should go about now pretending to raise the dead, pretending to cast out devils, we would regard him as insane. What, then, can we say of Christ? If we wish to save his reputation we are compelled to say that he never pretended to raise the dead; that he never claimed to have cast out devils.

We must take the ground that these ignorant and impossible things were invented by zealous disciples, who sought to deify their leader.

In those ignorant days these falsehoods added to the fame of Christ. But now they put his character in peril and belittle the authors of the gospels.

Can we now believe that water was changed into wine? John tells of this childish miracle, and says that the other disciples were present, yet Matthew, Mark and Luke say nothing about it.

Take the miracle of the man cured by the pool of Bethseda. John says that an angel troubled the waters of the pool of Bethseda, and that whoever got into the pool first after the waters were troubled was healed.

Does anybody now believe that an angel went into the pool and troubled the waters? Does anybody now think that the poor wretch who got in first was healed? Yet the author of the gospel according to John believed and asserted these absurdities. If he was mistaken about that, he may have been about all the miracles he records.

John is the only one who tells about this pool of Bethseda. Possibly the other disciples did not believe the story.

How can we account for these pretended miracles?

In the days of the disciples, and for many centuries after, the world was filled with the supernatural. Nearly everything that happened was regarded as miraculous. God was the immediate governor of the world. If the people were good, God sent seed time and harvest; but if they were bad he sent flood and hail, frost and famine. If anything wonderful happened it was exaggerated until it became a miracle.

Of the order of events—of the unbroken and the unbreakable chain of causes and effects—the people had no knowledge and no thought.

A miracle is the badge and brand of fraud. No miracle ever was performed. No intelligent, honest man ever pretended to perform a miracle, and never will.

If Christ had wrought the miracles attributed to him; if he had cured the palsied and insane; if he had given hearing to the deaf, vision to the blind; if he had cleansed the leper with a word, and with a touch had given life and feeling to the withered limb; if he had given pulse and motion, warmth and thought, to cold and breathless clay; if he had conquered death and rescued from the grave its pallid prey—no word would have been uttered, no hand raised, except in praise and honor. In his presence all heads would have been uncovered—all knees upon the ground.

Is it not strange that at the trial of Christ no one was found to say a word in his favor? No man stood forth and said: "I was a leper, and this man cured me with a touch." No woman said: "I am the widow of Nain and this is my son whom this man raised from the dead."

No man said: "I was blind, and this man gave me sight."
All silent.

THE PHILOSOPHY OF CHRIST

Millions assert that the philosophy of Christ is perfect—that he was the wisest that ever uttered speech.

Let us see:

Resist not evil. If smitten on one cheek turn the other.

Is there any philosophy, any wisdom in this? Christ takes from goodness, from virtue, from the truth, the right of self-defense. Vice becomes the master of the world, and the good become the victims of the infamous.

No man has the right to protect himself, his property, his wife and children. Government becomes impossible, and the world is at the mercy of criminals. Is there any absurdity beyond this?

Love your enemies.

Is this possible? Did any human being ever love his enemies? Did Christ love his, when he denounced them as whited sepulchers, hypocrites and vipers?

We cannot love those who hate us. Hatred in the hearts of others does not breed love in ours. Not to resist evil is absurd; to love your enemies is impossible.

Take no thought for the morrow.

The idea was that God would take care of us as he did of sparrows and lilies. Is there the least sense in that belief?

Does God take care of anybody?

Can we live without taking thought for the morrow? To plow, to sow, to cultivate, to harvest, is to take thought for the morrow. We plan and work for the future, for our children, for the unborn generations to come. Without this forethought there could be no progress, no civilization. The world would go back to the caves and dens of savagery.

If thy right eye offend thee, pluck it out. If thy right hand offend thee, cut it off.

Why? Because it is better that one of our members should perish than that the whole body should be cast into hell.

Is there any wisdom in putting out your eyes or cutting off your hands? Is it possible to extract from these extravagant sayings the smallest grain of common sense?

Swear not at all; neither by Heaven, for it is God's throne; nor by the Earth, for it is his footstool; nor by Jerusalem, for it is his holy city.

Here we find the astronomy and geology of Christ. Heaven is the throne of God, the monarch; the earth is his footstool. A footstool that turns over at the rate of a thousand miles an hour, and sweeps through space at the rate of over a thousand miles a minute! Where did Christ think heaven was? Why was Jerusalem a holy city? Was it because the inhabitants were ignorant, crud and superstitious?

If any man will sue thee at the law and take away thy coat let him have thy cloak also.

Is there any philosophy, any good sense, in that commandment? Would it not be just as sensible to say: "If a man obtains a judgment against you for one hundred dollars, give him two hundred."

Only the insane could give or follow this advice.

Think not I come to send peace on earth. I came not to send peace, but a sword. For I am come to set a man at variance against his father, and the daughter against her mother.

If this is true, how much better it would have been had he remained away.

Is it possible that he who said, "Resist not evil," came to bring a sword? That he who said, "Love your enemies," came to destroy the peace of the world?

To set father against son, and daughter against father—what a glorious mission!

He did bring a sword, and the sword was wet for a thousand years with innocent blood. In millions of hearts he sowed the seeds of hatred and revenge. He divided nations and families, put out the light of reason, and petrified the hearts of men.

And every one that hath forsaken house, or breathren, or sisters, or father, or mother, or wife, or children, or lands, for my name's sake, shall receive an hundredfold, and shall inherit everlasting life.

According to the writer of Matthew, Christ, the compassionate, the merciful, uttered these terrible words. Is it possible that Christ offered the bribe of eternal joy to those who would desert their fathers, their mothers, their wives and children? Are we to win the happiness of heaven by deserting the ones we love? Is a home to be ruined here for the sake of a mansion there?

And yet it is said that Christ is an example for all the

world. Did he desert his father and mother? He said, speaking to his mother: "Woman, what have I to do with thee?"

The Pharisees said unto Christ: "Is it lawful to pay tribute unto Caesar?"

Christ said: "Show me the tribute money." They brought him a penny. And he saith unto them: "Whose is the image and the superscription?" They said: "Caesar's." And Christ said: "Render unto Caesar the things that are Caesar's."

Did Christ think that the money belonged to Caesar because his image and superscription were stamped upon it? Did the penny belong to Caesar or to the man who had earned it? Had Caesar the right to demand it because it was adorned with his image?

Does it appear from this conversation that Christ understood the real nature and use of money?

Can we now say that Christ was the greatest of philosophers?

IS CHRIST OUR EXAMPLE?

He never said a word in favor of education. He never even hinted at the existence of any science. He never uttered a word in favor of industry, economy or of any effort to better our condition in this world. He was the enemy of the successful, of the wealthy. Dives was sent to hell, not because he was bad, but because he was rich. Lazarus went to heaven, not because he was good, but because he was poor.

Christ cared nothing for painting, for sculpture, for music—nothing for any art. He said nothing about the duties of nation to nation, of king to subject; nothing about the rights of man; nothing about intellectual liberty or the freedom of speech. He said nothing about the sacredness of home; not one word for the fireside; not a word in favor of marriage, in honor of maternity.

He never married. He wandered homeless from place to place with a few disciples. None of them seem to have been engaged in any useful business, and they seem to have lived on alms.

All human ties were held in contempt; this world was sacrificed for the next; all human effort was discouraged. God would support and protect.

At last, in the dusk of death, Christ, finding that he was mistaken, cried out: "My God My God! Why hast thou forsaken me?"

We have found that man must depend on himself. He must clear the land; he must build the home; he must plow and plant; he must invent; he must work with hand and brain; he must overcome the difficulties and obstructions; he must conquer and enslave the forces of nature to the end that they may do the work of the world.

WHY SHOULD WE PLACE CHRIST AT THE TOP AND SUMMIT OF THE HUMAN RACE?

Was he kinder, more forgiving, more self-sacrificing than Buddha? Was he wiser, did he meet death with more perfect calmness, than Socrates?   Was he more patient, more charitable, than Epictetus? Was he a greater philosopher, a deeper thinker, than Epicurus? In what respect was he the superior of Zoroaster? Was he gentler than Lao-tsze, more universal than Confucius? Were his ideas of human rights and duties superior to those of Zeno? Did he express grander truths than Cicero? Was his mind subtler than Spinoza's? Was his brain equal to Kepler's or Newton's?   Was he grander in death—a sublimer martyr than Bruno? Was he in intelligence, in the force and beauty of expression, in breadth and scope of thought, in wealth of illustration, in aptness of comparison, in knowledge of the human brain and heart, of all passions, hopes and fears, the equal of Shakespeare, the greatest of the human race?

If Christ was in fact God, he knew all the future. Before him like a panorama moved the history yet to be. He knew how his words would be interpreted. He knew what crimes, what horrors, what infamies, would be committed in his name. He knew that the hungry flames of persecution would climb around the limbs of countless martyrs. He knew that; thousands and thousands of brave men and women would languish in dungeons in darkness, filled with pain. He knew that his church would invent and use instruments of torture; that his followers would appeal to whip and fagot, to chain and rack. He saw the horizon of the future lurid with the flames of the auto da fe. He knew what creeds would spring like poisonous fungi from every text. He saw the ignorant sects waging war against each other. He saw thousands of men, under the orders of priests, building prisons for their fellow men. He saw thousands of scaffolds dripping with the best and bravest blood. He saw his followers using the instruments of pain. He heard the groans—saw the faces white with agony. He heard the shrieks and sobs and cries of all the moaning, martyred multitudes. He knew that commentaries would be written on his words with swords, to be read by the light of fagots. He knew that the Inquisition would be born of the teachings attributed to him.

He saw the interpolations and falsehoods that hypocrisy would write and tell. He saw all wars that would he waged, and he knew that above these fields of death, these dungeons, these rackings, these burnings, these executions, for a thousand years would float the dripping banner of the cross.

He knew that hypocrisy would be robed and crowned— that cruelty and credulity would rule the world; knew that liberty would perish from the earth; knew that popes and kings in his name would enslave the souls and bodies of men; knew that they would persecute and destroy the discoverers, thinkers and inventors; knew that his church would extinguish reason's holy light and leave the world without a star.

He saw his disciples extinguishing the eyes of men,

flaying them alive, cutting out their tongues, searching for all the nerves of pain.

He knew that in his name his followers would trade in human flesh; that cradles would be robbed and women's breasts unbabed for gold.

And yet he died with voiceless lips.

Why did he fail to speak? Why did he not tell his disciples, and through them the world: "You shall not burn, imprison and torture in my name. You shall not persecute your fellow-men."

Why did he not plainly say: "I am the Son of God," or, "I am God"? Why did he not explain the Trinity? Why did he not tell the mode of baptism that was pleasing to him? Why did he not write a creed? Why did he not break the chains of slaves? Why did he not say that the Old Testament was or was not the inspired word of God? Why did he not write the New Testament himself? Why did he leave his words to ignorance, hypocrisy and chance? Why did he not say something positive, definite and satisfactory about another world? Why did he not turn the tear-stained hope of heaven into the glad knowledge of another life? Why did he not tell us something of the rights of man, of the liberty of hand and brain?

Why did he go dumbly to his death, leaving the world to misery and to doubt?

I will tell you why. He was a man, and did not know.

INSPIRATION

Not before about the third century was it claimed or believed that the books composing the New Testament were inspired.

It will be remembered that there were a great number of books, of Gospels, Epistles and Acts, and that from these the "inspired" ones were selected by "uninspired" men.

Between the "Fathers" there were great differences of opinion as to which books were inspired; much discussion and plenty of hatred. Many of the books now deemed spurious were by many of the "Fathers" regarded as divine, and some now regarded as inspired were believed to be spurious. Many of the early Christians and some of the "Fathers" repudiated the Gospel of John, the Epistle to the Hebrews, Jade, James, Peter, and the Revelation of St. John. On the other hand, many of them regarded the Gospel of the Hebrews, of the Egyptians, the Preaching of Peter, the Shepherd of Hermas, the Epistle of Bar nabas, the Pastor of Hermas, the Revelation of Peter, the Revelation of Paul, the Epistle of Clement, the Gospel of Nicodemus, inspired books, equal to the very best.

From all these books, and many others, the Christians selected the inspired ones. The men who did the selecting were ignorant and superstitious. They were firm believers in the miraculous. They thought that diseases had been cured by the aprons and handkerchiefs of the apostles, by the bones of the dead. They believed in the fable of the Phoenix, and that the hyenas changed their sex every year.

Were the men who through many centuries made the selections inspired? Were they—ignorant, credulous, stupid and malicious—as well qualified to judge of "inspiration" as the students of our time? How are we bound by their opinion? Have we not the right to judge for ourselves?

Erasmus, one of the leaders of the Reformation, declared that the Epistle to the Hebrews was not written by Paul, and he denied the inspiration of Second and Third John, and also of Revelation. Luther was of the same opinion. He declared James to be an epistle of straw, and denied the inspiration of Revelation. Zwinglius rejected the book of Revelation, and even Calvin denied that Paul was the author of Hebrews.

The truth is that the Protestants did not agree as to what books are inspired until 1647, by the Assembly of Westminster.

To prove that a book is inspired you must prove the existence of God. You must also prove that this God thinks, acts, has objects, ends and aims. This is somewhat difficult.

It is impossible to conceive of an infinite being. Having no conception of an infinite being, it is impossible to tell whether all the facts we know tend to prove or disprove the existence of such a being.

God is a guess. If the existence of God is admitted, how are we to prove that he inspired the writers of the books of the Bible?

How can one man establish the inspiration of another? How can an inspired man prove that he is inspired? How can he know himself that he is inspired? There is no way to prove the fact of inspiration. The only evidence is the word of some man who could by no possibility know anything on the subject.

What is inspiration? Did God use men as instruments? Did he cause them to write his thoughts? Did he take possession of their minds and destroy their wills?

Were these writers only partly controlled, so that their mistakes, their ignorance and their prejudices were mingled with the wisdom of God?

How are we to separate the mistakes of man from the thoughts of God? Can we do this without being inspired ourselves? If the original writers were inspired, then the translators should have been, and so should be the men who tell us what the Bible means.

How is it possible for a human being to know that he is inspired by an infinite being? But of one thing we may be certain: An inspired book should certainly excel all the books produced by uninspired men. It should, above all, be true, filled with wisdom, blossoming in beauty—perfect.

Ministers wonder how I can be wicked enough to attack the Bible.

I will tell them: This book, the Bible, has persecuted, even unto death, the wisest and the best. This book stayed and stopped the onward movement of the human race. This book poisoned the fountains of learning and misdirected the energies of man.

This book is the enemy of freedom, the support of slavery. This book sowed the seeds of hatred in families and nations, fed the flames of war, and impoverished the world. This book is the breastwork of kings and tyrants—the enslaver of women and children. This book has corrupted parliaments and courts. This book has made colleges and universities the teachers of error and the haters of science. This book has filled Christendom with hateful, cruel, ignorant and warring sects. This book taught men to kill their fellows for religion's sake. This book funded the Inquisition, invented the instruments of torture, built the dungeons in which the good and loving languished, forged the chains that rusted in their flesh, erected the scaffolds whereon they died. This book piled fagots about the feet of the just. This book drove reason from the minds of millions and filled the asylums with the insane.

This book has caused fathers and mothers to shed the blood of their babes. This book was the auction block on which the slave-mother stood when she was sold from her child. This book filled the sails of the slave-trader and made merchandise of human flesh. This book lighted the fires that burned "witches" and "wizards." This book filled the darkness with ghouls and ghosts, and the bodies of men and women with devils. This book polluted the souls of men with the infamous dogma of eternal pain. This book made credulity the greatest of virtues, and investigation the greatest of crimes. This book filled nations with hermits, monks and nuns—with the pious and the useless. This book placed the ignorant and unclean saint above the philosopher and philanthropist. This book taught man to despise the joys of this life, that he might be happy in another—to waste this world for the sake of the next.

I attack this book because it is the enemy of human liberty—the greatest obstruction across the highway of human progress.

Let me ask the ministers one question: How can you be wicked enough to defend this book?

THE REAL BIBLE

For thousands of years men have been writing the real Bible, and it is being written from day to day, and it will never be finished while man has life. All the facts that we know, all the truly recorded events, all the discoveries and inventions, all the wonderful machines whose wheels and levers seem to think, all the poems, crystals from the brain, flowers from the heart, all the songs of love and joy, of smiles and tears, the great dramas of Imagination's world, the wondrous paintings, miracles of form and color, of light and shade, the marvelous marbles that seem to live and breathe, the secrets told by rock and star, by dust and flower, by rain and snow, by frost and flame, by winding stream and desert sand, by mountain range and billowed sea.

All the wisdom that lengthens and ennobles life, all that avoids or cures disease, or conquers pain—all just and perfect laws and rules that guide and shape our lives, all thoughts that feed the flames of love the music that transfigures, enraptures and enthralls the victories of heart and brain, the miracles that hands have wrought, the deft and cunning hands of those who worked for wife and child, the histories of noble deeds, of brave and useful men, of faithful loving wives, of quenchless mother-love, of conflicts for the right, of sufferings for the truth, of all the best that all the men and women of the world have said, and thought and done through all the years.

These treasures of the heart and brain—these are the Sacred Scriptures of the human race.

From *What Would You Substitute for the Bible as a Moral Guide?*

You ask me what I would "substitute for the Bible as a moral guide."

I know that many people regard the Bible as the only moral guide and believe that in that book only can be found the true and perfect standard of morality.

There are many good precepts, many wise sayings and many good regulations and laws in the Bible, and these are mingled with bad precepts, with foolish sayings, with absurd rules and cruel laws.

But we must remember that the Bible is a collection of many books written centuries apart, and that it in part represents the growth and tells in part the history of a people. We must also remember that the writers treat of many subjects. Many of these writers have nothing to say about right or wrong, about vice or virtue. ...

In Exodus we have an account of the manner in which Jehovah delivered the Jews from Egyptian bondage. We now know that the Jews were never enslaved by the Egyptians; that the entire story is a fiction. We know this, because there is not found in Hebrew a word of Egyptian origin, and there is not found in the language of the Egyptians a word of Hebrew origin. This being so, we know that the Hebrews and Egyptians could not have lived together for hundreds of years.

Certainly Exodus was not written to teach morality. In that book you cannot find one word against human slavery. As a matter of fact, Jehovah was a believer in that institution.

The killing of cattle with disease and hail, the murder of the firstborn, so that in every house was death, because the king refused to let the Hebrews go, certainly was not moral; it was fiendish. The writer of that book regarded all the people of Egypt, their children, their flocks and herds, as the property of Pharaoh, and these people and these cattle were killed, not because they had done anything wrong, but simply for the purpose of punishing the king. Is it possible to get any morality out of this history?

All the laws found in Exodus, including the Ten Commandments, so far as they are really good and sensible, were at that time in force among all the peoples of the world. … So men and women are not virtuous because of anything in books or creeds.

All the Ten Commandments that are good were old, were the result of experience. … Many of the regulations found in Exodus, Leviticus, Numbers and Deuteronomy, are good. Many are absurd and cruel.

The entire ceremonial of worship is insane.

Most of the punishment for violations of laws are unphilosophic and brutal. …

Nothing of a moral nature can be found in Joshua or Judges. These books are filled with crimes, with massacres and murders. They are about the same as the real history of the Apache Indians. …

There are some good Psalms, and there are some that are infamous. Most of these Psalms are selfish. Many of them are passionate appeals for revenge. ...

You can, by selecting passages from different books, make a very good creed, and by selecting passages from different books, you can make a very bad creed.

The trouble is that the spirit of the Old Testament, its disposition, its temperament, is bad, selfish and cruel. The most fiendish things are commanded, commended and applauded.

The stories that are told of Joseph, of Elisha, of Daniel and Gideon, and of many others, are hideous; hellish.

On the whole, the Old Testament cannot be considered a moral guide.

Jehovah was not a moral God. He had all the vices, and he lacked all the virtues. He generally carried out his threats, but he never faithfully kept a promise.

At the same time, we must remember that the Old Testament is a natural production, that it was written by savages who were slowly crawling toward the light. We must give them credit for the noble things they said, and we must be charitable enough to excuse their faults and even their crimes.

I know that many Christians regard the Old Testament as the foundation and the New as the superstructure, and while many admit that there are faults and mistakes in the Old Testament, they insist that the New is the flower and perfect fruit.

I admit that there are many good things in the New Testament, and if we take from that book the dogmas, of eternal pain, of infinite revenge, of the atonement, of human sacrifice, of the necessity of shedding blood; if we throw away the doctrine of non-resistance, of loving enemies, the idea that prosperity is the result of wickedness, that Poverty is a preparation for Paradise, if we throw all these away and take the good, sensible passages, applicable to conduct, then we can make a fairly good moral guide,—narrow but moral.

Of course, many important things would be left out. You would have nothing about human rights, nothing in favor of the family, nothing for education, nothing for investigation, for thought and reason, but still you would have a fairly good moral guide.

On the other hand, if you would take the foolish passages, the extreme ones, you could make a creed that would satisfy an insane asylum.

If you take the cruel passages, the verses that inculcate eternal hatred, verses that writhe and hiss like serpents, you can make a creed that would shock the heart of a hyena. ...

The Bible is not a moral guide.

Any man who follows faithfully all its teachings is an enemy of society and will probably end his days in a prison or an asylum.

What is morality?

In this world we need certain things. We have many wants. We are exposed to many dangers. We need food, fuel, raiment and shelter, and besides these wants, there is, what may be called, the hunger of the mind.

We are conditioned beings, and our happiness depends upon conditions. There are certain things that diminish, certain things that increase, well-being. There are certain things that destroy and there are others that preserve.

Happiness, including its highest forms, is after all the only good, and everything, the result of which is to produce or secure happiness, is good, that is to say, moral. Everything that destroys or diminishes well-being is bad, that is to say, immoral. In other words, all that is good is moral, and all that is bad is immoral.

What then is, or can be called, a moral guide? The shortest possible answer is one word: Intelligence.

We want the experience of mankind, the true history of the race. We want the history of intellectual development, of the growth of the ethical, of the idea of justice, of conscience, of charity, of self-denial. We want to know the paths and roads that have been traveled by the human mind.

These facts in general, these histories in outline, the results reached, the conclusions formed, the principles evolved, taken together, would form the best conceivable moral guide.

We cannot depend on what are called "inspired books," or the religions of the world. These religions are based on the supernatural, and according to them we are under obligation to worship and obey some supernatural being, or beings. All these religions are inconsistent with intellectual liberty. They are the enemies of thought, of investigation, of mental honesty. They destroy the manliness of man. They promise eternal rewards for belief, for credulity, for what they call faith.

These religions teach the slave virtues. They make inanimate things holy, and falsehoods sacred. They create artificial crimes. To eat meat on Friday, to enjoy yourself on Sunday, to eat on fast-days, to be happy in Lent, to dispute a priest, to ask for evidence, to deny a creed, to express your sincere thought, all these acts are sins, crimes against some god, To give your honest opinion about Jehovah, Mohammed or Christ, is far worse than to maliciously slander your neighbor. To question or doubt miracles is far worse than to deny known facts. Only the obedient, the credulous, the cringers, the kneelers, the meek, the unquestioning, the true believers, are regarded as moral, as virtuous. It is not enough to be honest, generous and useful; not enough to be governed by evidence, by facts. In addition to this, you must believe. These things are the foes of morality. They subvert all natural conceptions of virtue.

All "inspired books," teaching that what the supernatural commands is right, and right because commanded, and that what the supernatural prohibits is wrong, and wrong because prohibited, are absurdly unphilosophic.

And all "inspired books," teaching that only those who obey the commands of the supernatural are, or can be, truly virtuous, and that unquestioning faith will be rewarded with eternal joy, are grossly immoral.

Again I say: Intelligence is the only moral guide.

From *The Foundations of Faith*

THE OLD TESTAMENT

One of the foundation stones of our faith is the Old Testament. If that book is not true, if its authors were unaided men, if it contains blunders and falsehoods, then that stone crumbles to dust. ...

JEHOVAH

God the Father.

The Jehovah of the Old Testament is the God of the Christians. ...

Why should the Bible speak of this God as a man?—of his walking in the garden in the cool of the evening—of his talking, hearing and smelling? If he has no passions why is he spoken of as jealous, revengeful, angry, pleased and loving?

In the [Jewish] Bible, God is spoken of as a person in the form of man, journeying from place to place, as having a home and occupying a throne. These ideas have been abandoned, and now the Christian's God is the infinite, the incomprehensible, the formless, bodiless and passionless.

THE TRINITY

The New Testament informs us that Christ was the son of Joseph and the son of God, and that Mary was his mother.

How is it established that Christ was the son of God?

It is said that Joseph was told so in a dream by an angel.

But Joseph wrote nothing on that subject—said nothing so far as we know. Mary wrote nothing, said nothing. The angel that appeared to Joseph or that informed Joseph said nothing to anybody else. Neither has the Holy Ghost, the supposed father, ever said or written one word. We have received no information from the parties who could have known anything on the subject. We get all our facts from those who could not have known.

How is it possible to prove that the Holy Ghost was the father of Christ?

Who knows that such a being as the Holy Ghost ever existed?

How was it possible for Mary to know anything about the Holy Ghost?

How could Joseph know that he had been visited by an angel in a dream?

Could he know that the visitor was an angel? It all occurred in a dream and poor Joseph was asleep. What is the testimony of one who was asleep worth?

All the evidence we have is that somebody who wrote part of the New Testament says that the Holy Ghost was the father of Christ, and that somebody who wrote another part of the New Testament says that Joseph was the father of Christ.

Matthew and Luke give the genealogy and both show that Christ was the son of Joseph.

The "Incarnation" has to be believed without evidence. There is no way in which it can be established. It is beyond the reach and realm of reason. It defies observation and is independent of experience.

It is claimed not only that Christ was the Son of God, but that he was, and is, God.

Was he God before he was born? Was the body of Mary the dwelling place of God?

What evidence have we that Christ was God?

Somebody has said that Christ claimed that God was his father and that he and his father were one. We do not know who this somebody was and do not know from whom he received his information.

Somebody who was "inspired" has said that Christ was of the blood of David through his father Joseph.

This is all the evidence we have.

Can we believe that God, the creator of the Universe, learned the trade of a carpenter in Palestine, that he gathered a few disciples about him, and after teaching for about three years, suffered himself to be crucified by a few ignorant and pious Jews?

THE THEOLOGICAL CHRIST

In the New Testament we find the teachings and sayings of Christ. If we say that the book is inspired, then we must admit that Christ really said all the things attributed to him by the various writers. If the book is inspired we must accept it all. We have no right to reject the contradictory and absurd and accept the reasonable and good. We must take it all just as it is.

My own observation has led me to believe that men are generally consistent in their theories and inconsistent in their lives.

So, I think that Christ in his utterances was true to his theory, to his philosophy.

If I find in the Testament sayings of a contradictory character, I conclude that some of those sayings were never uttered by him. The sayings that are, in my judgment, in accordance with what I believe to have been his philosophy, I accept, and the others I throw away.

There are some of his sayings which show him to have been a devout Jew, others that he wished to destroy Judaism, others showing that he held all people except the Jews in contempt and that he wished to save no others, others showing that he wished to convert the world, still others showing that he was forgiving, self-denying and loving, others that he was revengeful and malicious, others, that he was an ascetic, holding all human ties in utter contempt.

The following passages show that Christ was a devout

Jew: "Swear not, neither by heaven, for it is God's throne, nor by the earth for it is his footstool, neither by Jerusalem for it is his holy city."

"Think not that I am come to destroy the law or the prophets, I am not come to destroy, but to fulfil."

"For after all these things, (clothing, food and drink) do the Gentiles seek."

So, when he cured a leper, he said: "Go thy way, show thyself unto the priest and offer the gift that Moses commanded."

Jesus sent his disciples forth saying: "Go not into the way of the Gentiles, and into any city of the Samaritans enter ye not, but go rather to the lost sheep of the house of Israel."

A woman came out of Canaan and cried to Jesus: "Have mercy on me, my daughter is sorely vexed with a devil"—but he would not answer. Then the disciples asked him to send her away, and he said: "I am not sent but unto the lost sheep of the house of Israel."

Then the woman worshiped him and said: "Lord help me." But he answered and said: "It is not meet to take the children's bread and cast it unto dogs." Yet for her faith he cured her child.

So, when the young man asked him what he must do to be saved, he said: "Keep the commandments."

Christ said: "The scribes and the Pharisees sit in Moses' seat, all therefore whatsoever they bid you observe, that observe and do."

"And it is easier for heaven and earth to pass, than one

tittle of the law to fail."

Christ went into the temple and cast out them that sold and bought there, and said: "It is written, my house is the house of prayer: but ye have made it a den of thieves."

"We know what we worship for salvation is of the Jews."

Certainly all these passages were written by persons who regarded Christ as the Messiah.

Many of the sayings attributed to Christ show that he was an ascetic, that he cared nothing for kindred, nothing for father and mother, nothing for brothers or sisters, and nothing for the pleasures of life.

Christ said to a man: "Follow me." The man said: "Suffer me first to go and bury my father." Christ answered: "Let the dead bury their dead." Another said: "I will follow thee, but first let me go bid them farewell which are at home."

Jesus said: "No man having put his hand to the plough, and looking back is fit for the kingdom of God. If thine right eye offend thee pluck it out. If thy right hand offend thee cut it off."

One said unto him: "Behold thy mother and thy brethren stand without, desiring to speak with thee." And he answered: "Who is my mother, and who are my brethren?" Then he stretched forth his hand toward his disciples and said: "Behold my mother and my brethren.

"And every one that hath forsaken houses, or brethren or sisters, or father or mother, or wife or children, or lands for my name's sake shall receive an hundred fold and shall inherit everlasting life."

"He that loveth father or mother more than me is not worthy of me; and he that loveth son or daughter more than me is not worthy of me."

Christ it seems had a philosophy.

He believed that God was a loving father, that he would take care of his children, that they need do nothing except to rely implicitly on God.

"Blessed are the merciful: for they shall obtain mercy.

"Love your enemies, bless them that curse you, do good to them that hate you and pray for them which despitefully use you and persecute you."

"Take no thought for your life, what ye shall eat or what ye shall drink, nor yet for your body, what ye shall put on. ... For your heavenly Father knoweth that ye have need of all these things."

"Ask and it shall be given you. Whatsoever ye would that men should do to you, do ye even so to them. If ye forgive men their trespasses your heavenly Father will also forgive you. The very hairs of your head are all numbered."

Christ seemed to rely absolutely on the protection of God until the darkness of death gathered about him, and then he cried: "My God! my God! why hast thou forsaken me?"

While there are many passages in the New Testament showing Christ to have been forgiving and tender, there are many others showing that he was exactly the opposite.

What must have been the spirit of one who said: "I am come to send fire on the earth? Suppose ye that I am come to give peace on earth? I tell you, nay, but rather division. For from henceforth there shall be five in one house divided, three against two, and two against three.   The father shall be divided against the son, and the son against the father, the mother against the daughter and the daughter against the mother, the mother-in-law against her daughter-in-law, and the daughter-in-law against her mother-in-law."

From *The Gods*

An honest God is the Noblest Work of Man.

Each nation has created a god, and the god has always resembled his creators. He hated and loved what they hated and loved, and he was invariably found on the side of those in power. Each god was intensely patriotic, and detested all nations but his own. All these gods demanded praise, flattery, and worship. Most of them were pleased with sacrifice, and the smell of innocent blood has ever been considered a divine perfume. All these gods have insisted upon having a vast number of priests, and the priests have always insisted upon being supported by the people, and the principal business of these priests has been to boast about their god, and to insist that he could easily vanquish all the other gods put together.

These gods have been manufactured after numberless models... Some have a thousand arms, some a hundred heads, some are adorned with necklaces of living snakes, some are armed with clubs, some with sword and shield, some with bucklers, and some have wings as a cherub; some were invisible, some would show themselves entire, and some would only show their backs; some were jealous, some were foolish, some turned themselves into men, some into swans, some into bulls, some into doves, and some into Holy Ghosts, and made love to the beautiful daughters of men. Some were married—all ought to have been—and some were considered as old bachelors from all eternity. Some had children, and the children were turned into gods and worshiped as their fathers had been. Most of these gods were revengeful, savage, lustful, and ignorant. As they generally depended upon their priests for information, their ignorance can hardly excite our astonishment.

These gods did not even know the shape of the worlds they had created, but supposed them perfectly flat. Some thought the day could be lengthened by stopping the sun, that the blowing of horns could throw down the walls of a city, and all knew so little of the real nature of the people they had created, that they commanded the people to love them. Some were so ignorant as to suppose that man could believe just as he might desire, or as they might command, and that to be governed by observation, reason, and experience was a most foul and damning sin. None of these gods could give a true account of the creation of this little earth. All were woefully deficient in geology and astronomy. As a rule, they were most miserable legislators, and as executives, they were far inferior to the average of American presidents.

These deities have demanded the most abject and degrading obedience. In order to please them, man must lay his very face in the dust. Of course, they have always been partial to the people who created them, and have generally shown their partiality by assisting those people to rob and destroy others, and to ravish their wives and daughters.

Nothing is so pleasing to these gods as the butchery of unbelievers. Nothing so enrages them, even now, as to have someone deny their existence.

Few nations have been so poor as to have but one god. Gods were made so easily, and the raw material cost so little, that generally the god market was fairly glutted, and heaven crammed with these phantoms. These gods not only attended to the skies, but were supposed to interfere in all the affairs of men. They presided over everybody and everything. They attended to every department. All was supposed to be under their immediate control. Nothing was too small—nothing too large; the falling of sparrows and the motions of the planets were alike attended to by these industrious and observing deities. From their starry thrones they frequently came to earth for the purpose of imparting information to man. It is related of one that he came amid thunderings and lightnings in order to tell the people that they should not cook a kid in its mother's milk. Some left their shining abodes to tell women that they should, or should not, have children, to inform a priest how to cut and wear his apron, and to give directions as to the proper manner of cleaning the intestines of a bird.

When the people failed to worship one of these gods, or failed to feed and clothe his priests, (which was much the same thing,) he generally visited them with pestilence and famine. Sometimes he allowed some other nation to drag them into slavery—to sell their wives and children; but generally he glutted his vengeance by murdering their firstborn. The priests always did their whole duty, not only in predicting these calamities, but in proving, when they did happen, that they were brought upon the people because they had not given quite enough to them.

These gods differed just as the nations differed... Each of these gods promised happiness here and hereafter to all his slaves, and threatened to eternally punish all who either disbelieved in his existence or suspected that some other god might be his superior; but to deny the existence of all gods was, and is, the crime of crimes. Redden your hands with human blood; blast by slander the fair fame of the innocent; strangle the smiling child upon its mother's knees; deceive, ruin and desert the beautiful girl who loves and trusts you, and your case is not hopeless. For all this, and for all these you may be forgiven. For all this, and for all these, that bankrupt court established by the gospel, will give you a discharge; but deny the existence of these divine ghosts, of these gods, and the sweet and tearful face of Mercy becomes livid with eternal hate. Heaven's golden gates are shut, and you, with an infinite curse ringing in your ears, with the brand of infamy upon your brow, commence your endless wanderings in the lurid gloom of hell—an immortal vagrant—an eternal outcast—a deathless convict.

One of these gods, and one who demands our love, our admiration and our worship, and one who is worshiped, if mere heartless ceremony is worship, gave to his chosen people for their guidance, the following laws of war: "When thou comest nigh unto a city to fight against it, then proclaim peace unto it. And it shall be if it make thee answer of peace, and open unto thee, then it shall be that all the people that is found therein shall be tributaries unto thee, and they shall serve thee. And if it will make no peace with thee, but will make war against thee, then thou shalt besiege it. And when the Lord thy God hath delivered it into thy hands, thou shalt smite every male thereof with the edge of the sword. But the women and the little ones, and the cattle, and all that is in the city, even all the spoil thereof, shalt thou take unto thyself, and thou shalt eat the spoil of thine enemies which the Lord thy God hath given thee. Thus shalt thou do unto all the cities which are very far off from thee, which are not of the cities of these nations. But of the cities of these people which the Lord thy God doth give thee for an inheritance, thou shalt save alive nothing that breatheth."

Is it possible for man to conceive of anything more perfectly infamous? Can you believe that such directions were given by any being except an infinite fiend? Remember that the army receiving these instructions was one of invasion. Peace was offered upon condition that the people submitting should be the slaves of the invader; but if any should have the courage to defend their homes, to fight for the love of wife and child, then the sword was to spare none—not even the prattling, dimpled babe.

And we are called upon to worship such a God; to get upon our knees and tell him that he is good, that he is merciful, that he is just, that he is love. We are asked to stifle every noble sentiment of the soul, and to trample under foot all the sweet charities of the heart. Because we refuse to stultify ourselves—refuse to become liars—we are denounced, hated, traduced and ostracized here, and this same god threatens to torment us in eternal fire the moment death allows him to fiercely clutch our naked helpless souls. Let the people hate, let the god threaten—we will educate them, and we will despise and defy the god.

The book, called the Bible, is filled with passages equally horrible, unjust and atrocious. This is the book to be read in schools in order to make our children loving, kind and gentle! This is the book they wish to be recognized in our Constitution as the source of all authority and justice! ...

We are asked to justify these frightful passages, these infamous laws of war, because the Bible is the word of God. As a matter of fact, there never was, and there never can be, an argument even tending to prove the inspiration of any book whatever. In the absence of positive evidence, analogy and experience, argument is simply impossible, and at the very best, can amount only to a useless agitation of the air. The instant we admit that a book is too sacred to be doubted, or even reasoned about, we are mental serfs. It is infinitely absurd to suppose that a god would Address a communication to intelligent beings, and yet make it a crime, to be punished in eternal flames, for them to use their intelligence for the purpose of understanding his communication. If we have the right to use our reason, we certainly have the right to act in accordance with it, and no god can have the right to punish us for such action.

The doctrine that future happiness depends upon belief is monstrous. It is the infamy of infamies. The notion that faith in Christ is to be rewarded by an eternity of bliss, while a dependence upon reason, observation and experience merits everlasting pain, is too absurd for refutation, and can be relieved only by that unhappy mixture of insanity and ignorance, called "faith." What man, who ever thinks, can believe that blood can appease God? And yet, our entire system of religion is based upon that believe. The Jews pacified Jehovah with the blood of animals, and according to the Christian system, the blood of Jesus softened the heart of God a little, and rendered possible the salvation of a fortunate few. It is hard to conceive how the human mind can give assent to such terrible ideas, or how any sane man can read the Bible and still believe in the doctrine of inspiration. ...

As long as man believes the Bible to be infallible, that book is his master. The civilization of this century is not the child of faith, but of unbelief—the result of free thought.

All that is necessary, as it seems to me, to convince any reasonable person that the Bible is simply and purely of human invention—of barbarian invention—is to read it. Read it as you would any other book; think of it as you would of any other; get the bandage of reverence from your eyes; drive from your heart the phantom of fear; push from the throne of your brain the coiled form of superstition—then read the Holy Bible, and you will be amazed that you ever, for one moment, supposed a being of infinite wisdom, goodness and purity, to be the author of such ignorance and of such atrocity.

Our ancestors not only had their god-factories, but they made devils as well. These devils were generally disgraced and fallen gods. Some had headed unsuccessful revolts; some had been caught sweetly reclining in the shadowy folds of some fleecy cloud, kissing the wife of the god of gods. These devils generally sympathized with man. There is in regard to them a most wonderful fact: In nearly all the theologies, mythologies and religions, the devils have been much more humane and merciful than the gods. No devil ever gave one of his generals an order to kill children and to rip open the bodies of pregnant women. Such barbarities were always ordered by the good gods. The pestilences were sent by the most merciful gods. The frightful famine, during which the dying child with pallid lips sucked the withered bosom of a dead mother, was sent by the loving gods. No devil was ever charged with such fiendish brutality.

One of these gods, according to the account, drowned an entire world with the exception of eight persons. The old, the young, the beautiful and the helpless were remorsely devoured by the shoreless sea. This, the most fearful tragedy that the imagination of ignorant priests ever conceived, was the act, not of a devil, but of a god, so-called, whom men ignorantly worship unto this day. What a stain such an act would leave upon the character of a devil! One of the prophets of one of these gods, having in his power a captured king, hewed him in pieces in the sight of all the people. Was ever any imp of any devil guilty of such savagery?

One of these gods is reported to have given the following directions concerning human slavery: "If thou buy a Hebrew servant, six years shall he serve, and in the seventh he shall go out free for nothing. If he came in by himself, he shall go out by himself; if he were married, then his wife shall go out with him. If his master have given him a wife, and she have borne him sons or daughters, the wife and her children shall be her master's, and he shall go out by himself. And if the servant shall plainly say, I love my master, my wife and my children; I will not go out free. Then his master shall bring him unto the judges: he shall also bring him unto the door, or unto the doorpost; and his master shall bore his ear through with an awl; and he shall serve him forever."

According to this, a man was given liberty upon condition that he would desert forever his wife and children. Did any devil ever force upon a husband, upon a father, so cruel and so heartless an alternative? Who can worship such a god? Who can bend the knee to such a monster? Who can pray to such a fiend?

All these gods threatened to torment forever the souls of their enemies. Did any devil ever make so infamous a threat? The basest thing recorded of the devil, is what he did concerning Job and his family, and that was done by the express permission of one of these gods, and to decide a little difference of opinion between their serene highnesses as to the character of "my servant Job."

The first account we have of the devil is found in that purely scientific book called Genesis, and is as follows: "Now the serpent was more subtle than any beast of the field which the Lord God had made, and he said unto the woman, Yea, hath God said, Ye shall not eat of the fruit of the trees of the garden? And the woman said unto the serpent, We may eat of the fruit of the trees of the garden; but of the fruit of the tree which is in the midst of the garden God hath said, Ye shall not eat of it, neither shall ye touch it, lest ye die. And the serpent said unto the woman, Ye shall not surely die. For God doth know that in the day ye eat thereof, then your eyes shall be opened and ye shall be as gods, knowing good and evil. And when the woman saw that the tree was good for food, and that it was pleasant to the eyes, and a tree to be desired to make one wise, she took of the fruit thereof and did eat, and gave also unto her husband with her, and he did eat. ... And the Lord God said, Behold the man is become as one of us, to know good and evil; and now, lest he put forth his hand, and take also of the tree of life: and eat, and live forever. Therefore the Lord God sent him forth from the Garden of Eden to till the ground from which he was taken. So he drove out the man, and he placed at the east of the Garden of Eden cherubim and a flaming sword, which turned every way to keep the way of the tree of life."

According to this account the promise of the devil was fulfilled to the very letter, Adam and Eve did not die, and they did become as gods, knowing good and evil.

The account shows, however, that the gods dreaded education and knowledge then just as they do now. The church still faithfully guards the dangerous tree of knowledge, and has exerted in all ages her utmost power to keep mankind from eating the fruit thereof. The priests have never ceased repeating the old falsehood and the old threat: "Ye shall not eat of it, neither shall ye touch it, lest ye die." From every pulpit comes the same cry, born of the same fear: "Lest they eat and become as gods, knowing good and evil." For this reason, religion hates science, faith detests reason, theology is the sworn enemy of philosophy, and the church with its flaming sword still guards the hated tree, and like its supposed founder, curses to the lowest depths the brave thinkers who eat and become as gods.

If the account given in Genesis is really true, ought we not, after all, to thank this serpent? He was the first schoolmaster, the first advocate of learning, the first enemy of ignorance, the first to whisper in human ears the sacred word liberty, the creator of ambition, the author of modesty, of inquiry, of doubt, of investigation, of progress and of civilization.

Give me the storm and tempest of thought and action, rather than the dead calm of ignorance and faith! Banish me from Eden when you will; but first let me eat of the fruit of the tree of knowledge! ...

To me, it seems easy to account for these ideas concerning gods and devils. They are a perfectly natural production. Man has created them all, and under the same circumstances would create them again. Man has not only created all these gods, but he has created them out of the materials by which he has been surrounded. Generally he has modeled them after himself, and has given them hands, heads, feet, eyes, ears, and organs of speech. Each nation made its gods and devils speak its language not only, but put in their mouths the same mistakes in history, geography, astronomy, and in all matters of fact, generally made by the people. No

god was ever in advance of the nation that created him. The
negroes represented their deities with black skins and curly
hair. The Mongolian gave to his a yellow complexion and
dark almond-shaped eyes. The Jews ware not allowed to
paint theirs, or we should have seen Jehovah with a full beard,
an oval face, and an aquiline nose. Zeus was a perfect Greek,
and Jove looked as though a member of the Roman senate.
The gods of Egypt had the patient face and placid look of the
loving people who made them.   The gods of northern
countries were represented warmly clad in robes of fur; those
of the tropics were naked. The gods of India were often
mounted upon elephants; those of some islanders were great
swimmers, and the deities of the Arctic zone were
passionately fond of whale's blubber. Nearly all people have
carved or painted representations of their gods, and these
representations were, by the lower classes, generally treated
as the real gods, and to these images and idols they addressed
prayers and offered sacrifice.

In some countries, even at this day, if the people after
long praying do not obtain their desires, they turn their images
off as impotent gods, or upbraid them in a most reproachful
manner, loading them with blows and curses 'How now, dog
of a spirit,' they say, 'we give you lodging in a magnificent
temple, we gild you with gold, feed you with the choicest
food, and offer incense to you; yet, after all this care, you are
so ungrateful as to refuse us what we ask.' Hereupon they
will pull the god down and drug him through the filth of the
street. If, in the meantime, it happens that they obtain their

request, then, with a great deal of ceremony, they wash him clean, carry him back and place him in his temple again, where they fall down and make excuses for what they have done. 'Of a truth,' they say, 'we were a little too hasty, and you were a little too long in your grant. Why should you bring this beating on yourself. But what is done cannot be undone. Let us not think of it any more. If you will forget what is past we will gild you over brighter again than before."

Man has never been at a loss for gods. He has worshiped almost everything, including the vilest and most disgusting beasts. He has worshiped fire, earth, air, water, light, stars, and for hundreds of ages prostrated himself before enormous snakes. Savage tribes often make gods of articles they get from civilized people. The Todas worship a cow-bell. The Kotas worship two silver plates, which they regard as husband and wife, and another tribe manufactured a god out of a king of hearts.

Man, having always been the physical superior of woman, accounts for the fact that most of the high gods have been males. Had woman been the physical superior, the powers supposed to be the rulers of Nature would have been women, and instead of being represented in the apparel of man, they would have luxuriated in trains, low necked dresses, laces and back hair.

Nothing can be plainer than that each nation gives to its god its peculiar characteristics, and that every individual gives to his god his personal peculiarities. ...

Man, in his ignorance, supposed that all phenomena were

produced by some intelligent powers, and with direct reference to him. To preserve friendly relations with these powers was, and still is, the object of all religions. Man knelt through fear and to implore assistance, or though gratitude for some favor which he supposed had been rendered. He endeavored by supplication to appease some being who, for some reason, had, as he believed, become enraged. The lightning and thunder terrified him. In the presence of the volcano he sank upon his knees. The great forests filled with wild and ferocious beasts, the monstrous serpents crawling in mysterious depths, the boundless sea, the flaming comets, the sinister eclipses, the awful calmness of the stars, and, more than all, the perpetual presence of death, convinced him that he was the sport and prey of unseen and malignant powers. The strange and frightful diseases to which he was subject, the freezing and burnings of fever, the contortions of epilepsy, the sudden palsies, the darkness of night, and the wild, terrible and fantastic dreams that filled his brain, salified him that he was haunted and pursued by countless spirits of evil. For some reason he supposed that these spirits differed in power—that they were not all alike malevolent—that the higher controlled the lower, and that his very existence depended upon gaining the assistance of the more powerful. For this purpose he resorted to prayer, to flattery, to worship and to sacrifice. These ideas appear to have been almost universal in savage man.

For ages all nations supposed that the sick and insane were possessed by evil spirits. For thousands of years the practice of medicine consisted in frightening these spirits away. Usually the priests would make the loudest and most discordant noises possible. They would blow horns, beat upon rude drums, clash cymbals, and in the meantime utter the most unearthly yells. If the noise remedy failed, they would implore the aid of some more powerful spirit.

To pacify these spirits was considered of infinite importance. The poor barbarian, knowing that men could be softened by gifts, gave to these spirits that which to him seemed of the most value. With bursting heart he would offer the blood of his dearest child. It was impossible for him to conceive of a god utterly unlike himself, and he naturally supposed that these powers of the air would be affected a little at the sight of so great and so deep a sorrow. It was with the barbarian then as with the civilized now—one class lived upon and made merchandise of the fears of another. Certain persons took it upon themselves to appease the gods, and to instruct the people in their duties to these unseen powers. This was the origin of the priesthood. The priest pretended to stand between the wrath of the gods and the helplessness of man. He was man's attorney at the court of heaven. He carried to the invisible world a flag of truce, a protest and a request. He came back with a command, with authority and with power. Man fell upon his knees before his own servant, and the priest, taking advantage of the awe inspired by his supposed influence with the gods, made of his fellowman a cringing hypocrite and slave. Even Christ, the supposed son of God, taught that persons were possessed of evil spirits, and frequently, according to the account, gave proof of his divine origin and mission by frightening droves of devils out of his unfortunate countrymen. Casting out devils was his principal employment, and the devils thus banished generally took occasion to acknowledge him as the true Messiah; which was not only very kind of them, but quite fortunate for him. The religious people have always regarded the testimony of these devils as perfectly conclusive and the writers of the New Testament quote the words of these imps of darkness with great satisfaction.

The fact that Christ could withstand the temptations of the devil was considered as conclusive evidence that he was assisted by some god, or at least by some being superior to man. St. Matthew gives an account of an attempt made by the devil to tempt the supposed son of God; and it has always excited the wonder of Christians that the temptation was so nobly and heroically withstood. The account to which I refer is as follows:

"Then was Jesus led up of the spirit into the wilderness to be tempted of the devil. And when the tempter came to him, he said: 'If thou be the son of God, command that these stones be made bread.' But he answered, and said: 'It is written: man shall not live by bread alone, but by every word that proceedeth out of the mouth of God.' Then the devil taketh him up into the holy city and setteth him upon a pinnacle of the temple and saith unto him: 'If thou be the son of God, cast thyself down; for it is written, He shall give his angels charge concerning thee, lest at any time thou shalt dash thy foot against a stone.' Jesus said unto him: 'It is written again, thou shalt not tempt the Lord thy God.' Again the devil taketh him up into an exceeding high mountain and sheweth him all the kingdoms of the world and the glory of them, and saith unto him: 'All these will I give thee if thou wilt fall down and worship me.'"

The Christians now claim that Jesus was God. If he was God, of course the devil knew that fact, and yet, according to this account, the devil took the omnipotent God and placed him upon a pinnacle of the temple, and endeavored to induce him to dash himself against the earth. Failing in that, he took the creator, owner and governor of the universe up into an exceeding high mountain and offered him this world—this grain of sand—if he, the God of all the worlds, would fall down and worship him, a poor devil, without even a tax title to one foot of dirt! Is it possible the devil was such an idiot? Should any great credit be given to this deity fear not being caught with such chaff? Think of it! The devil—the prince of sharpers—the king of cunning—the master of finesse, trying to bribe God with a grain of sand that belonged to God! ...

We are told that the universe was designed and created, and that it is absurd to suppose that matter has existed from eternity, but that it is perfectly self-evident that a god has.

If a god created the universe, then, there must have been a time when he commenced to create. Back of that time there must have been an eternity, during which there had existed nothing—absolutely nothing—except this supposed god. According to this theory, this god spent an eternity, so to speak, in an infinite vacuum, and in perfect idleness.

Admitting that a god did create the universe, the question then arises, of what did he create it? It certainly was not made of nothing. Nothing considered in the light of a raw material is a most decided failure. It follows, then that the god must have made the universe out of himself, he being the only existence. The universe is material, and if it was made of god, the god must have been material. ...

From *Heretics And Hericies*

LIBERTY, A WORD WITHOUT WHICH ALL WORDS ARE VAIN

Whoever has an opinion of his own, and honestly expresses it, will be guilty of heresy. Heresy is what the minority believe; it is the name given by the powerful to the doctrine of the weak. This word was born of the hatred, arrogance and cruelty of those who love their enemies, and who, when smitten on one cheek, turn the other. This word was born of intellectual slavery in the feudal ages of thought. It was an epithet used in the place of argument. From the commencement of the Christian era, every art has been exhausted and every conceivable punishment inflicted to force all people to hold the same religious opinions. This effort was born of the idea that a certain belief was necessary to the salvation of the soul. Christ taught, and the church still teaches, that unbelief is the blackest of crimes. God is supposed to hate with an infinite and implacable hatred, every heretic upon the earth, and the heretics who have died are supposed at this moment to be suffering the agonies of the damned. The church persecutes the living and her God burns, for all eternity, the dead.

It is claimed that God wrote a book called the Bible, and it is generally admitted that this book is somewhat difficult to understand. As long as the church had all the copies of this book, and the people were not allowed to read it, there was comparatively little heresy in the world; but when it was printed and read, people began honestly to differ as to its meaning. A few were independent and brave enough to give the world their real thoughts, and for the extermination of these men the church used all her power. Protestants and Catholics vied with each other in the work of enslaving the human mind. For ages they were rivals in the infamous effort to rid the earth of honest people. They infested every country, every city, town, hamlet and family. They appealed to the worst passions of the human heart. They sowed the seeds of discord and hatred in every land. Brother denounced brother, wives informed against their husbands, mothers accused their children, dungeons were crowded with the innocent; the flesh of the good and true rotted in the clasp of chains; the flames devoured the heroic, and in the name of the most merciful God, his children were exterminated with famine, sword, and fire. Over the wild waves of battle rose and fell the banner of Jesus Christ. For sixteen hundred years the robes of the church were red with innocent blood. The ingenuity of Christians was exhausted in devising punishment severe enough to be inflicted upon other Christians who honestly and sincerely differed with them upon any point whatever.

Give any orthodox church the power, and today they would punish heresy with whip, and chain, and fire. As long as a church deems a certain belief essential to salvation, just so long it will kill and burn if it has the power. Why should the church pity a man whom her God hates? Why should she show mercy to a kind and noble heretic whom her God will burn in eternal fire? Why should a Christian be better than his God? It is impossible for the imagination to conceive of a greater atrocity than has been perpetrated by the church. Every nerve in the human body capable of pain has been sought out and touched.

Let it be remembered that all churches have persecuted heretics to the fullest extent of their power. Toleration has increased only when and where the power of the church has diminished. From Augustine until now the spirit of the Christians has remained the same. There has been the same intolerance, the same undying hatred of all who think for themselves, and the same determination to crush out of the human brain all knowledge inconsistent with an ignorant creed.

Every church pretends that it has a revelation from God, and that this revelation must be given to the people through the church; that the church acts through its priests, and that ordinary mortals must be content with a revelation—not from God—but from the church. Had the people submitted to this preposterous claim, of course there could have been but one church, and that church never could have advanced. It might have retrograded, because it is not necessary to think or investigate in order to forget. Without heresy there could have been no progress.

The highest type of the orthodox Christian does not forget; neither does he learn. He neither advances nor recedes. He is a living fossil embedded in that rock called faith. He makes no effort to better his condition, because all his strength is exhausted in keeping other people from improving theirs. The supreme desire of his heart is to force all others to adopt his creed, and in order to accomplish this object he denounces free thinking as a crime, and this crime he calls heresy. When he had power, heresy was the most terrible and formidable of words.   It meant confiscation, exile, imprisonment, torture, and death.

In those days the cross and rack were inseparable companions. Across the open Bible lay the sword and fagot. Not content with burning such heretics as were alive, they even tried the dead, in order that the church might rob their wives and children.   The property of all heretics was confiscated, and on this account they charged the dead with being heretical—indicted, as it were, their dust—to the end that the church might clutch the bread of orphans. Learned divines discussed the propriety of tearing out the tongues of heretics before they were burned, and the general opinion was, that this ought to be done so that the heretics should not be able, by uttering blasphemies, to shock the Christians who were burning them.   With a mixture of ferocity and Christianity, the priests insisted that heretics ought to be burned at a slow fire, giving as a reason that more time was given them for repentance.

No wonder that Jesus Christ said, "I came not to bring peace, but a sword."

Every priest regarded himself as the agent of God. He answered all questions by authority, and to treat him with disrespect was an insult offered to God. No one was asked to think, but all were commanded to obey.

In 1208 the Inquisition was established. Seven years afterward, the fourth council of the Lateran enjoined all kings and rulers to swear an oath that they would exterminate heretics from their dominions. The sword of the church was unsheathed, and the world was at the mercy of ignorant and infuriated priests, whose eyes feasted upon the agonies they inflicted. Acting, as they believed, or pretended to believe, under the command of God; stimulated by the hope of infinite reward in another world—hating heretics with every drop of their bestial blood; savage beyond description; merciless beyond conception,—these infamous priests, in a kind of frenzied joy, leaped upon the helpless victims of their rage. They crushed their bones in iron boots; tore their quivering flesh with iron hooks and pincers; cut off their lips and eyelids; pulled out their nails, and into the bleeding quick thrust needles; tore out their tongues; extinguished their eyes; stretched them upon racks; flayed them alive; crucified them with their heads downward; exposed them to wild beasts; burned them at the stake; mocked their cries and groans; robbed their children, and then prayed God to finish the holy work in hell.

Millions upon millions were sacrificed upon the altars of bigotry. The Catholic burned the Lutheran, the Lutheran burned the Catholic, the Episcopalian tortured the Presbyterian, the Presbyterian tortured the Episcopalian. Every denomination killed all it could of every other; and each Christian felt in duty bound to exterminate every other Christian who denied the smallest fraction of his creed.

In the reign of Henry VIII—that pious and moral founder of the apostolic Episcopal Church—there was passed by the parliament of England an act entitled "An act for abolishing of diversity of opinion." And in this act was set forth what a good Christian was obliged to believe:

First, That in the sacrament was the real body and blood of Jesus Christ.

Second, That the body and blood of Jesus Christ was in the bread, and the blood and body of Jesus Christ was in the wine.

Third, That priests should not marry.

Fourth, That vows of chastity were of perpetual obligation.

Fifth, That private masses ought to be continued; and,

Sixth, That auricular confession to a priest must be maintained.

This creed was made by law, in order that all men might know just what to believe by simply reading the statute. The church hated to see the people wearing out their brains in thinking upon these subjects. It was thought far better that a creed should be made by parliament, so that whatever might be lacking in evidence might be made up in force. The punishment for denying the first article was death by fire. For the denial of any other article, imprisonment, and for the second offence—death.

Your attention is called to these six articles, established

during the reign of Henry VIII, and by the Church of England, simply because not one of these articles is believed by that church today. If the law then made by the church could he enforced now, every Episcopalian would be burned at the stake.

Similar laws were passed in most Christian countries, as all orthodox churches firmly believed that mankind could be legislated into heaven. According to the creed of every church, slavery leads to heaven, liberty leads to hell. It was claimed that God had founded the church, and that to deny the authority of the church was to be a traitor to God, and consequently an ally of the devil. To torture and destroy one of the soldiers of Satan was a duty no good Christian cared to neglect. Nothing can be sweeter than to earn the gratitude of God by killing your own enemies. Such a mingling of profit and revenge, of heaven for yourself and damnation for those you dislike, is a temptation that your ordinary Christian never resists.

According to the theologians, God, the Father of us all, wrote a letter to his children. The children have always differed somewhat as to the meaning of this letter. In consequence of these honest differences, these brothers began to cut out each other's hearts. In every land, where this letter from God has been read, the children to whom and for whom it was written have been filled with hatred and malice. They have imprisoned and murdered each other, and the wives and children of each other. In the name of God every possible crime has been committed, every conceivable outrage has been perpetrated. Brave men, tender and loving women, beautiful girls, and prattling babes have been exterminated in the name of Jesus Christ. For more than fifty generations the church has carried the black flag. Her vengeance has been measured only by her power. During all these years of infamy no heretic has ever been forgiven. With the heart of a fiend she has hated; with the clutch of avarice she has grasped; with the jaws of a dragon she has devoured; pitiless as famine, merciless as fire, with the conscience of a serpent: such is the history of the Church of God.

I do not say, and I do not believe, that Christians are as bad as their creeds. In spite of church and dogma, there have been millions and millions of men and women true to the loftiest and most generous promptings of the human heart. They have been true to their convictions, and, with a self-denial and fortitude excelled by none, have labored and suffered for the salvation of men. Imbued with the spirit of self-sacrifice, believing that by personal effort they could rescue at least a few souls from the infinite shadow of hell, they have cheerfully endured every hardship and scorned every danger. And yet, notwithstanding all this, they believed that honest error was a crime. They knew that the Bible so declared, and they believed that all unbelievers would be eternally lost. They believed that religion was of God, and all heresy of the devil. They killed heretics in defense of their own souls and the souls of their children. They killed them because, according to their idea, they were the enemies of God, and because the Bible teaches that the blood of the unbeliever is a most acceptable sacrifice to heaven.

Nature never prompted a loving mother to throw her child into the Ganges. Nature never prompted men to exterminate each other for a difference of opinion concerning the baptism of infants. These crimes have been produced by religions filled with all that is illogical, cruel and hideous. These religions were produced for the most part by ignorance, tyranny and hypocrisy. Under the impression that the infinite ruler and creator of the universe had commanded the destruction of heretics and infidels, the church perpetrated all these crimes.

Men and women have been burned for thinking there is but one God; that there was none; that the Holy Ghost is younger than God; that God was somewhat older than his son; for insisting that good works will save a man without faith; that faith will do without good works; for declaring that a sweet babe will not be burned eternally, because its parents failed to have its head wet by a priest; for speaking of God as though he had a nose; for denying that Christ was his own father; for contending that three persons, rightly added together, make more than one; for believing in purgatory; for denying the reality of hell; for pretending that priests can forgive sins; for preaching that God is an essence; for denying that witches rode through the air on sticks; for doubting the total depravity of the human heart; for laughing at irresistible grace, predestination and particular redemption; for denying that good bread could be made of the body of a dead man; for pretending that the pope was not managing this world for

God, and in the place of God; for disputing the efficacy of a vicarious atonement; for thinking the Virgin Mary was born like other people; for thinking that a man's rib was hardly sufficient to make a good- sized woman; for denying that God used his finger for a pen; for asserting that prayers are not answered, that diseases are not sent to punish unbelief; for denying the authority of the Bible; for having a Bible in their possession; for attending mass, and for refusing to attend; for wearing a surplice; for carrying a cross, and for refusing; for being a Catholic, and for being a Protestant; for being an Episcopalian, a Presbyterian, a Baptist, and for being a Quaker. In short, every virtue has been a crime, and every crime a virtue. The church has burned honesty and rewarded hypocrisy. And all this, because it was commanded by a book—a book that men had been taught implicitly to believe, long before they knew one word that was in it. They had been taught that to doubt the truth of this book—to examine it, even—was a crime of such enormity that it could not be forgiven, either in this world or in the next.

The Bible was the real persecutor. The Bible burned heretics, built dungeons, founded the Inquisition, and trampled upon all the liberties of men.

How long, O how long will mankind worship a book? How long will they grovel in the dust before the ignorant legends of the barbaric past? How long, O how long will they pursue phantoms in a darkness deeper than death?

Unfortunately for the world, about the beginning of the sixteenth century, a man by the name of Gerard Chauvin was married to Jeanne Lefranc, and still more unfortunately for the world, the fruit of this marriage was a son, called John Chauvin, who afterwards became famous as John Calvin, the founder of the Presbyterian Church.

... This man, when in the flush of youth, was elected to the office of preacher in Geneva. He at once, in union with Farel, drew up a condensed statement of the Presbyterian doctrine, and all the citizens of Geneva, on pain of banishment, were compelled to take an oath that they believed this statement. Of this proceeding Calvin very innocently remarked that it produced great satisfaction. A man named Caroli had the audacity to dispute with Calvin. For this outrage he was banished.

To show you what great subjects occupied the attention of Calvin, it is only necessary to state that he furiously discussed the question as to whether the sacramental bread should be leavenéd or unleavened. He drew up laws regulating the cut of the citizens' clothes, and prescribing their diet, and all those whose garments were not in the Calvin fashion were refused the sacrament. At last, the people becoming tired of this petty theological tyranny, banished Calvin. In a few years, however, he was recalled and received with great enthusiasm. After this he was supreme, and the will of Calvin became the law of Geneva.

Under his benign administration, James Gruet was beheaded because he had written some profane verses. The slightest word against Calvin or his absurd doctrines was punished as a crime.

In 1553 a man was tried at Vienna by the Catholic Church for heresy. He was convicted and sentenced to death by burning. It was apparently his good fortune to escape. Pursued by the sleuth hounds of intolerance he fled to Geneva for protection. A dove flying from hawks, sought safety in the nest of a vulture. This fugitive from the cruelty of Rome asked shelter from John Calvin, who had written a book in favor of religious toleration. Serviettes had forgotten that this book was written by Calvin when in the minority; that it was written in weakness to be forgotten in power; that it was produced by fear instead of principle. He did not know that Calvin had caused his arrest at Vienna, in France, and had sent a copy of his work, which was claimed to be blasphemous, to the archbishop. He did not then know that the Protestant Calvin was acting as one of the detectives of the Catholic Church, and had been instrumental in procuring his conviction for heresy. Ignorant of all this unspeakable infamy, he put himself in the power of this very Calvin. The maker of the Presbyterian creed caused the fugitive Serviettes to be arrested for blasphemy. He was tried. Calvin was his accuser. He was convicted and condemned to death by fire. On the morning of the fatal day, Calvin saw him, and Serviettes, the victim, asked forgiveness of Calvin, the murderer. Serviettes was bound to the stake, and the fagots were lighted. The wind carried the flames somewhat away from his body, so that he slowly roasted for hours. Vainly he implored a speedy death. At last the flames climbed round his form; through smoke and fire his murderers saw a white heroic face. And there they watched until a man became a charred and shriveled mass.

Liberty was banished from Geneva, and nothing but Presbyterianism was left. Honor, justice, mercy, reason and charity were all exiled; but the five points of predestination, particular redemption, irresistible grace, total depravity, and the certain perseverance of the saints remained instead.

Calvin founded a little theocracy, modeled after the Old Testament, and succeeded in erecting the most detestable government that ever existed, except the one from which it was copied. ...

The doctrines of Calvin spread rapidly, and were eagerly accepted by multitudes on the continent; but Scotland, in a few years, became the real fortress of Presbyterianism. The Scotch succeeded in establishing the same kind of theocracy that flourished in Geneva. The clergy took possession and control of everybody and everything. It is impossible to exaggerate the mental degradation, the abject superstition of the people of Scotland during the reign of Presbyterianism. Heretics were hunted and devoured as though they had been wild beasts. The gloomy insanity of Presbyterianism took possession of a great majority of the people. They regarded their ministers as the Jews did Moses and Aaron. They believed that they were the especial agents of God, and that whatsoever they bound in Scotland would be bound in heaven. There was not one particle of intellectual freedom. No man was allowed to differ with the church, or to even contradict a priest. Had Presbyterianism maintained its ascendancy, Scotland would have been peopled by savages today.

The revengeful spirit of Calvin took possession of the Puritans, and caused them to redden the soil of the New World with the brave blood of honest men. Clinging to the five points of Calvin, they too established governments in accordance with the teachings of the Old Testament. They too attached the penalty of death to the expression of honest thought. They too believed their church supreme, and exerted all their power to curse this continent with a spiritual despotism as infamous as it was absurd. They believed with Luther that universal toleration is universal error, and universal error is universal hell. Toleration was denounced as a crime.

Fortunately for us, civilization has had a softening effect even upon the Presbyterian Church. ...

The cry of "heresy" has been growing fainter and fainter, and, as a consequence, the ministers of that denomination have ventured, now and then, to express doubts as to the damnation of infants, and the doctrine of total depravity. ...

From *Inspiration Of Bible*

A FEW REASONS FOR DOUBTING THE INSPIRATION
OF THE BIBLE

The Old Testament must have been written nearly two
thousand years before the invention of Printing. There were
but few copies, and these were in the keeping of those whose
interest might have prompted interpolations, and whose
ignorance might have led to mistakes.

The written Hebrew was composed entirely of
consonants, without any points or marks standing for vowels,
so that anything like accuracy was impossible. Anyone can
test this for himself by writing an English sentence, leaving
out the vowels. It will take far more inspiration to read than
to write a book with consonants alone.

The books composing the Old Testament were not
divided into chapters or verses, and no system of punctuation
was known. Think of this a moment and you will see how
difficult it must be to read such a book.

There was not among the Jews any dictionary of their
language, and for this reason the accurate meaning of words
could not be preserved. Now the different meanings of words
are preserved so that by knowing the age in which a writer

lived we can ascertain with reasonable certainty his meaning.

The Old Testament was printed for the first time in 1488. Until this date it existed only in manuscript, and was constantly exposed to erasures and additions.

It is now admitted by the most learned in the Hebrew language that in our present English version of the Old Testament there are at least one hundred thousand errors. Of course the believers in inspiration assert that these errors are not sufficient in number to cast the least suspicious upon any passages upholding what are called the "fundamentals."

It is not certainly known who in fact wrote any of the books of the Old Testament. For instance, it is now generally conceded that Moses was not the author of the Pentateuch.

Other books, not now in existence, are referred to in the Old Testament as of equal authority, such as the books of Jasher, Nathan, Ahijah, Iddo, Jehu, Sayings of the Seers.

The Christians are not agreed among themselves as to what books are inspired. The Catholics claim as inspired the books of Maccabees, Tobit, Esdras, etc. Others doubt the inspiration of Esther, Ecclesiastes, and the Song of Solomon.

In the book of Esther and the Song of Solomon the name of God is not mentioned, and no reference is made to any supreme being, nor to any religions duty. These omissions would seem sufficient to cast a little doubt upon these books.

Within the present century [the late 1800s] manuscript copies of the Old Testament have been found throwing new light and changing in many instances the present readings. In consequence a new version is now being made by a theological syndicate composed of English and American divines, and after this is published it may be that our present Bible will fall into disrepute.

The fact that language is continually changing that words are constantly dying and others being born; that the same word has a variety of meanings during its life, shows how hard it is to preserve the original ideas that might have been expressed in the Scriptures, for thousands of years, without dictionaries, without the art of printing, and without the light of contemporaneous literature.

Whatever there was of the Old Testament seems to have been lost from the time of Moses until the days of Josiah, and it is probable that nothing like the Bible existed in any permanent form among the Jews until a few hundred years before Christ. It is said that Ezra gave the Pentateuch to the Jews, but whether he found or originated it is unknown. So it is claimed that Nehemiah gathered up the manuscripts about the kings and prophets, while the books of Job, Psalms, Proverbs, Ruth, Ecclesiastes, and some others were either collected or written long after. The Jews themselves did not agree as to what books were really inspired.

In the Old Testament we find several contradictory laws about the same thing, and contradictory accounts of the same occurrences. In the twentieth chapter of Exodus we find the first account of the giving of Ten Commandments. In the thirty-fourth chapter another account is given. These two accounts could never have been written by the same person. Read these two accounts and you will be forced to admit that one of them cannot be true. So there are two histories of the creation, of the flood, and of the manner in which Saul became king.

It is now generally admitted that Genesis must have been written by two persons, and the parts written by each can be separated, and when separated they are found to contradict each other in many important particulars.

It is also admitted that copyists made verbal changes not only, but pieced out fragments; that the speeches of Elihu in the book of Job were all interpolated, and that most of the prophecies were made by persons whose names we have never known.

The manuscripts of the Old Testament were not alike, and the Greek version differed from the Hebrew, and there was no absolutely received text of the Old Testament until after the commencement of the Christian era. Marks and points to denote vowels were invented probably about the seventh century after Christ. Whether these vowels were put in the proper places or not is still an open question.

No one in the world has learning enough, nor has the time enough even if he had the learning, and could live a thousand years, to find out what books really belong to and constitute the Old Testament, the authors these books, when they were written, and what they mean. And until a man has the learning and the time to do all this he cannot certainly tell whether he believe Bible or not.

If a revelation from God was actually necessary to the happiness of man here and to his salvation hereafter, it is not easy to see why such revelation was not given to all the nations of the earth. Why were the millions of Asia, Egypt, and America left to the insufficient light of nature. Why was not a written, or what is still better, printed revelation given to Adam and Eve in the Garden of Eden? And why were the Jews themselves without a Bible until the days of Ezra the scribe? Why was nature not so made that it would give light enough? Why did God make men and leave them in darkness—a darkness that he knew would fill the world with want and crime, and crowd with damned souls the dungeons of hell? Were the Jews the only people who needed a revelation? It may be said that God had no time to waste with other nations, and gave the Bible to the Jews that other

nations through them might learn of his existence and his will.
If he wished other nations to be informed, and revealed
himself to but one, why did he not choose a people that
mingled with others? Why did he give the message to those
who had no commerce, who were obscure and unknown, and
who regarded other nations with the hatred born of bigotry
and weakness? What would we now think of a God who
made his will known to the South Sea Islanders for the benefit
of the civilized world? If it was of such vast importance for
man to know that there is a God, why did not God make
himself known? This fact could have been revealed by an
infinite being instantly to all, and there certainly was no
necessity of telling it alone to the Jews, and allowing millions
for thousands of years to die in utter ignorance.

... [Many peoples] are substantially ignorant of the
Bible. ... There are hundreds of languages and tongues in
which no Bible has yet been printed. Why did God allow, and
why does he still allow, a vast majority of his children to
remain in ignorance of his will?

If the Bible is the foundation of all civilization, of all just
ideas of right and wrong, of our duties to God and each other,
why did God not give to each nation at least one copy to start
with? He must have known that no nation could get along
successfully without a Bible, and he also knew that man could
not make one for himself. Why, then, were not the books
furnished? He must have known that the light of nature was

not sufficient to reveal the scheme of the atonement, the necessity of baptism, the immaculate conception, transubstantiation, the arithmetic of the Trinity, or the resurrection of the dead.

It is probably safe to say that not one-third of the inhabitants of this world ever heard of the Bible, and not one-tenth ever read it. It is also safe to say that no two persons who ever read it agreed as to its meaning, and it is not likely that even one person has ever understood it. Nothing is more needed at the present time than an inspired translator. Then we shall need an inspired commentator, and the translation and the commentary should be written in an inspired universal language, incapable of change, and then the whole world should be inspired to understand this language precisely the same. Until these things are accomplished, all written revelations from God will fill the world with contending sects, contradictory creeds and opinions.

All persons who know anything of constitutions and laws know how impossible it is to use words that will convey the same ideas to all. The best statesmen, the profoundest lawyers, differ as widely about the real meaning of treaties and statutes as do theologians about the Bible. When the differences of lawyers are left to courts, and the courts give written decisions, the lawyers will again differ as to the real meaning of the opinions. Probably no two lawyers in the United States understand our Constitution alike. To allow a few men to tell what the Constitution means, and to hang for treason all who refuse to accept the opinions of these few men, would accomplish in politics what most churches have asked for in religion.

The idea that the universe was made in six days, and is but about six thousand years old, is too absurd for serious refutation. Neither will it do to say that the six days were six periods, because this does away with the Sabbath, and is in direct violation of the text.

Neither is it reasonable that this God made man out of dust, and woman out of one of the ribs of the man; that this pair were put in a garden; that they were deceived by a snake that had the power of speech; that they were turned out of this garden to prevent them from eating of the tree of life and becoming immortal; that God himself made them clothes; that the sons of God intermarried with the daughters of men; that to destroy all life upon the earth a flood was sent that covered the highest mountains; that Noah and his sons built an ark and saved some of all animals as well as themselves; that the people tried to build a tower that would reach to heaven; that God confounded their language, and in this way frustrated their design.

It is hard to believe that God talked to Abraham as one man talks to another; that he gave him land that he pointed out; that he agreed to give him land that he never did; that he ordered him to murder his own son; that angels were in the habit of walking about the earth eating veal dressed with butter and milk, and making bargains about the destruction of cities.

Certainly a man ought not to be eternally damned for entertaining an honest doubt about a woman having been turned into a pillar of salt, about cities being destroyed by storms of fire and brimstone, and about people once having lived for nearly a thousand years.

One can scarcely be blamed for hesitating to believe that God met Moses at a hotel and tried to kill him; [Ex. iv, 24.] that afterward he made this same Moses a god to Pharaoh, and gave him his brother Aaron for a prophet; [Ex. vii, 1.] that he turned all the ponds and pools and streams and all the rivers into blood, [Ex. viii, 19.] and all the water in vessels of wood and stone; that the rivers thereupon brought forth frogs; [Ex. viii, 3 that the frogs covered the whole land of Egypt; that he changed dust into lice, so that all the men, women, children, and animals were covered with them; [Ex. viii, 16, 17.] that he sent swarms of flies upon the Egyptians; [Ex. viii, 21.] that he destroyed the innocent cattle with painful diseases; that he covered man and beast with blains and boils; [Ex. ix, 9.] that he so covered the magicians of Egypt with boils that they could not stand before Moses for the purpose of performing the same feat; [Ex. xii, 11.] that he destroyed every beast and every man that was in the fields, and every herb, and broke every tree with storm of hail and fire; [Ex. ix, 25.] that he sent locusts that devoured every herb that escaped the hail, and devoured every tree that grew; [Ex. x, 15.] that he caused thick darkness over the land and put lights in the houses of the Jews; [Ex. x, 22, 23.] that he destroyed all of the firstborn of Egypt, from the firstborn of Pharaoh upon the throne to the firstborn of the maidservant that sat behind the mill, [Ex. xi, 5.] together with the firstborn of all beasts, so that there was not a house in which the dead were not. [Ex. xii, 29.]

It is very hard to believe that three millions of people left a country and marched twenty or thirty miles all in one day. To notify so many people would require a long time, and then the sick, the halt, and the old would be apt to impede the march.   It seems impossible that such a vast number—six hundred thousand men, besides women and children—could have been cared for, could have been fed and clothed, and the sick nursed, especially when we take into consideration that "they were thrust out of Egypt, and could not tarry, neither had they prepared for themselves any victual." [Ex. xii, 37-39.]

It seems cruel to punish a man forever for denying that God went before the Jews by day "in a pillar of a cloud to lead them the way, and by night in a pillar of fire to give them light to go by day and night," or for denying that Pharaoh pursued the Jews with six hundred chosen chariots, and all the chariots of Egypt, and that the six hundred thousand men of

war of the Jews were sore afraid when they saw the pursuing
hosts. It does seems strange that after all the water in a
country had been turned to blood—after it had been overrun
with frogs and devoured with flies; after all the cattle had died
with the murrain, and the rest had been killed by the fire and
hail and the remainder had suffered with boils, and the
firstborn of all that were left had died; that after locusts had
devoured every herb and eaten up every tree of the field, and
the firstborn had died, from the firstborn of the king on the
throne to the firstborn of the captive in the dungeon; that after
three millions of people had left, carrying with them the
jewels of silver and gold and the raiment of their oppressors,
the Egyptians still had enough soldiers and chariots and
horses left to pursue and destroy an army of six hundred
thousand men, if God had not interfered.

It certainly ought to satisfy God to torment a man for four
or five thousand years for insisting that it is but a small thing
for an infinite being to vanquish an Egyptian army; that it was
rather a small business to trouble people with frogs, flies, and
vermin; that it looked almost malicious to cover people with
boils and afflict cattle with disease; that a real good God
would not torture innocent beasts on account of something the
owners had done; that it was absurd to do miracles before a
king to induce him to act in a certain way, and then harden his
heart so that he would refuse; and that to kill all the firstborn
of a nation was the act of a heartless fiend.

Why should a man, because he has done a bad action, go and kill a sheep? How can man make friends with God by cutting the throats of bullocks and goats? Why should God delight in the shedding of blood? Why should he want his altar sprinkled with blood, and the horns of his altar tipped with blood, and his priests covered with blood? Why should burning flesh be a sweet savor in the nostrils of God? Why did he compel his priests to be butchers, cutters and stabbers? Why should the same God kill a man for eating the fat of an ox, a sheep, or a goat?

Could it be a consolation to a man when dying to think that he had always believed that God told Aaron to take two goats and draw cuts to see which goat should be killed and which should be a scapegoat? [Lev. xvi, 8.] And that upon the head of the scapegoat Aaron should lay both his hands and confess over him all the iniquities of the children of Israel, and all their transgressions, and put them all on the head of the goat, and send him away by the hand of a fit man into the wilderness; and that the goat should bear upon him all the iniquities of the people into a land not inhabited? [Lev. xvi, 21, 22.] How could a goat carry away a load of iniquities and transgressions? Why should he carry them to a land uninhabited? Were these sins contagious? About how many sins could an average goat carry? Could a man meet such a goat now without laughing?

Why should God object to a man wearing a garment

made of woolen and linen? Why should he care whether a man rounded the corners of his beard? [Lev. xix, 19, 27.] Why should God prevent a man from offering the sacred, bread merely because he had a flat nose, or was lame, or had five fingers on one hand, or had a broken foot, or was a dwarf? If he objected to such people, why did he make them? [Lev. xxi, 18-20.]

How, in the desert of Sinai, did the Jews obtain curtains of fine linen? How did these absconding slaves make cherubs of gold? Where did they get the skins of badgers, and how did they dye them red? How did they make wreathed chains and spoons, basins and tongs? Where did they get the blue cloth and their purple? Where did they get the sockets of brass? How did they coin the shekel of the sanctuary? How did they overlay boards with gold? Where did they get the numberless instruments and tools necessary to accomplish all these things? Where did they get the fine flour and the oil? Were all these found in the desert of Sinai? Is it a sin to ask these questions? Are all these doubts born of a malignant and depraved heart? Why should God in this desert prohibit priests from drinking wine, and from eating moist grapes? How could these priests get wine?

Do not these passages show that these laws were made long after the Jews had left the desert, and that they were not given from Sinai? Can you imagine a God silly enough to tell a horde of wandering savages upon a desert that they must not eat any fruit of the trees they planted until the fourth year?

Can any sane man believe that the sun stood still in the midst of heaven and hasted not to go down about a whole day, and that the moon stayed? [Josh. x, 13.] That these miracles were performed in the interest of massacre and bloodshed; that the Jews destroyed men, women, and children by the million, and practiced every cruelty that the ingenuity of their God could suggest? Is it possible that these things really happened? Is it possible that God commanded them to be done? Again I ask you to read the book of Joshua. After reading all its horrors you will feel a grim satisfaction in the dying words of Joshua to the children of Israel: "Know for a certainty that the Lord your God will no more drive out any of these nations from before you; but they shall be snares and traps unto you, and scourges in your sides, and thorns in your eyes, until ye perish from off this good land." [Josh. xiii, 13.]

Think of a God who boasted that he gave the Jews a land for which they did not labor, cities which they did not build, and allowed them to eat of olive-yards and vineyards which they did not plant. [Josh. xxiv, 13.] Think of a God who murders some of his children for the benefit of the rest, and then kills the rest because they are not thankful enough. Think of a God who had the power to stop the sun and moon, but could not defeat an army that had iron chariots. [Judges 1, 19.]

Read the story of Jephthah and his daughter, and then tell me what you think of a father who would sacrifice his daughter to God, and what you think of a God who would receive such a sacrifice. This one story should be enough to make every tender and loving father hold this book in utter abhorrence. Is it necessary, in order to be saved, that one must believe that an angel of God appeared unto Manoah in the absence of her husband; that this angel afterward went up in a flame of fire; that as a result of this visit a child was born whose strength was in his hair? a child that made beehives of lions, incendiaries of foxes, and had a wife that wept seven days to get the answer to his riddle? Will the wrath of God abide forever upon a man for doubting the story that Samson killed a thousand men with a new jawbone? Is there enough in the Bible to save a soul with this story left out? Is hell hungry for those who deny that water gashed from a "hollow place" in a dry bone? Is it evidence of a new heart to believe that one man turned over a house so large that over three thousand people were on the roof?

For my part, I cannot believe these things, and if my salvation depends upon my credulity I am as good as damned already. I cannot believe that the Philistines took back the ark with a present of five gold mice, and that thereupon God relented. [1 Sam. vi, 4.] I cannot believe that God killed fifty thousand men for looking into a box. [1 Sam. vi, 19.] It seems incredible, after all the Jews had done, after all their wars and victories, even when Saul was king, that there was not among them one smith who could make a sword or spear, and that they were compelled to go to the Philistines to sharpen every plowshare, coulter, and mattock. [1 Sam.xiii,

19, 20.] Can you believe that God said to Saul, "Now go and smite Amalek, and utterly destroy all that they have, and spare them not; but slay both man and woman, infant and suckling"? Can you believe that because Saul took the king alive after killing every other man, woman, and child, the ogre called Jehovah was displeased and made up his mind to hurl Saul from the throne and give his place to another? [1 Sam. xv.] I cannot believe that the Philistines all ran away because one of their number was killed with a stone. I cannot justify the conduct of Abigail, the wife of Nabal, who took presents to David. David hardly did right when he said to this woman, "I have hearkened to thy voice, and have accepted thy person." It could hardly have been chance that made Nabal so deathly sick next morning and killed him in ten days. All this looks wrong, especially as David married his widow before poor Nabal was fairly cold.

I cannot believe that Solomon passed all the kings of the earth in riches; that all the kings of the earth sought his presence and brought presents of silver and gold, raiment, harness, spices, and mules—a rate year by year. [2 Chron. ix, 22-24.] Is it possible that Shishak, a King of Egypt, invaded Palestine with seventy thousand horsemen and twelve hundred chariots of war? [2 Chron. xii, 2, 3.] I cannot believe that in a battle between Jeroboam and Abijah, the army of Abijah actually slew in one day five hundred thousand chosen men. [2 Chron. xiv, 17.] Does anyone believe that Zerah, the Ethiopian, invaded Palestine with a million men? [2 Chron.

xiv, 9.] I cannot believe that Jehoshaphat had a standing army of nine hundred and sixty thousand men. [2 Chron. xvii, 14-19.] I cannot believe that God advertised for a liar to act as his messenger. [2 Chron. xviii, 19- 22.] I cannot believe that King Amaziah did right in the sight of the Lord, and that he broke in pieces ten thousand men by casting them from a precipice. [2 Chron. xxv, 12.] I cannot think that God smote a king with leprosy because he tried to burn incense. [2 Chron. xxvi, 19.] I cannot think that Pekah slew one hundred and twenty thousand men in one day. [2 Chron. xxviii, 6.]

From *The Jews*

When I was a child, I was taught that the Jews were an exceedingly hard-hearted and cruel people, and that they were so destitute of the finer feelings that they had a little while before that time crucified the only perfect man who had appeared upon the earth; that this perfect man was also perfect God, and that the Jews had really stained their hands with the blood of the Infinite.

When I got somewhat older, I found that nearly all people had been guilty of substantially the same crime—that is, that they had destroyed the progressive and the thoughtful; that religionists had in all ages been cruel; that the chief priests of all people had incited the mob, to the end that heretics—that is to say, philosophers—that is to say, men who knew that the chief priests were hypocrites—might be destroyed.

I also found that Christians had committed more of these crimes than all other religionists put together.

I also became acquainted with a large number of Jewish people, and I found them like other people, except that, as a rule, they were more industrious, more temperate, had fewer vagrants among them, no beggars, very few criminals; and in addition to all this, I found that they were intelligent, kind to their wives and children, and that, as a rule, they kept their contracts and paid their debts.

The prejudice was created almost entirely by religious, or

rather irreligious, instruction. All children in Christian countries are taught that all the Jews are to be eternally damned who die in the faith of Abraham, Isaac and Jacob, that it is not enough to believe in the inspiration of the Old Testament—not enough to obey the Ten Commandments— not enough to believe the miracles performed in the days of the prophets, but that every Jew must accept the New Testament and must be a believer in Christianity—that is to say, he must be regenerated—or he will simply be eternal kindling wood.

The church has taught, and still teaches, that every Jew is an outcast; that he is today busily fulfilling prophecy; that he is a wandering witness in favor of "the glad tidings of great joy;" that Jehovah is seeing to it that the Jews shall not exist as a nation—that they shall have no abiding place, but that they shall remain scattered, to the end that the inspiration of the Bible may be substantiated.

Dr. John Hall of this city, a few years ago, when the Jewish people were being persecuted in Russia, took the ground that it was all fulfillment of prophecy, and that whenever a Jewish maiden was stabbed to death, God put a tongue in every wound for the purpose of declaring the truth of the Old Testament.

Just as long as Christians take these positions, of course they will do what they can to assist in the fulfillment of what they call prophecy, and they will do their utmost to keep the Jewish people in a state of exile, and then point to that fact as one of the cornerstones of Christianity.

My opinion is that in the early days of Christianity all sensible Jews were witnesses against the faith, and in this way excited the hostility of the orthodox. Every sensible Jew knew that no miracles had been performed in Jerusalem. They all knew that the sun had not been darkened, that the graves had not given up their dead, that the veil of the temple had not been rent in twain—and they told what they knew. They were then denounced as the most infamous of human beings, and this hatred has pursued them from that day to this.

There is no other chapter in history so infamous, so bloody, so cruel, so relentless, as the chapter in which is told the manner in which Christians—those who love their enemies—have treated the Jewish people. This story is enough to bring the blush of shame to the cheek, and the words of indignation to the lips of every honest man.

Nothing can be more unjust than to generalize about nationalities, and to speak of a race as worthless or vicious, simply because you have met an individual who treated you unjustly. There are good people and bad people in all races, and the individual is not responsible for the crimes of the nation, or the nation responsible for the actions of the few. Good men and honest men are found in every faith, and they are not honest or dishonest because they are Jews or Gentiles, but for entirely different reasons.

Some of the best people I have ever known are Jews, and some of the worst people I have known are Christians. The Christians were not bad simply because they were Christians, neither were the Jews good because they were Jews. A man is far above these badges of faith and race. Good Jews are precisely the same as good Christians, and bad Christians are wonderfully like bad Jews.

Personally, I have either no prejudices about religion, or I have equal prejudice against all religions. The consequence is that I judge of people not by their creeds, not by their rites, not by their mummeries, but by their actions.

In the first place, at the bottom of this prejudice lies the coiled serpent of superstition. In other words, it is a religious question. It seems impossible for the people of one religion to like the people believing in another religion. They have different gods, different heavens, and a great variety of hells. For the followers of one god to treat the followers of another god decently is a kind of treason. In order to be really true to his god, each follower must not only hate all other gods, but the followers of all other gods.

The Jewish people should outgrow their own superstitions. It is time for them to throw away the idea of inspiration. The intelligent Jew of today knows that the Old Testament was written by barbarians, and he knows that the rites and ceremonies are simply absurd. He knows that no intelligent man should care anything about Abraham, Isaac and Jacob, three dead barbarians. In other words, the Jewish people should leave their superstition and rely on science and philosophy.

The Christian should do the same. He, by this time, should know that his religion is a mistake, that his creed has no foundation in the eternal verities. The Christian certainly should give up the hopeless task of converting the Jewish people, and the Jews should give up the useless task of converting the Christians. There is no propriety in swapping superstitions—neither party can afford to give any boot.

When the Christian throws away his cruel and heartless superstitions, and when the Jew throws away his, then they can meet as man to man.

In the meantime, the world will go on in its blundering way, and I shall know and feel that everybody does as he must, and that the Christian, to the extent that he is prejudiced, is prejudiced by reason of his ignorance, and that consequently the great lever with which to raise all mankind into the sunshine of philosophy, is intelligence.

From *Some Mistakes Of Moses*

For many years I have regarded the Pentateuch simply as a record of a barbarous people, in which are found a great number of the ceremonies of savagery, many absurd and unjust laws, and thousands of ideas inconsistent with known and demonstrated facts.

To me it seemed almost a crime to teach that this record was written by inspired men; that slavery, polygamy, wars of conquest and extermination were right, and that there was a time when men could win the approbation of infinite Intelligence, Justice, and Mercy, by violating maidens and by butchering babes. To me it seemed more reasonable that savage men had made these laws. ...

Were we allowed to read the Bible as we do all other books, we would admire its beauties, treasure its worthy thoughts, and account for all its absurd, grotesque and cruel things, by saying that its authors lived in rude, barbaric times. But we are told that it was written by inspired men; that it contains the will of God; that it is perfect, pure, and true in all its parts; the source and standard of all moral and religious truth; that it is the star and anchor of all human hope; the only guide for man, the only torch in Nature's night. These claims are so at variance with every known recorded fact, so palpably absurd, that every free, unbiased soul is forced to raise the standard of revolt.

HE WHO ENDEAVORS TO CONTROL THE MIND BY
FORCE IS A TYRANT, HE WHO SUBMITS IS A SLAVE.

I want to do what little I can to ... broaden the
intellectual horizon of our people, to destroy the prejudices
born of ignorance and fear, to do away with the blind worship
of the ignoble past, with the idea that all the great and good
are dead, that the living are totally depraved, that all pleasures
are sins, that sighs and groans are alone pleasing to God, that
thought is dangerous, that intellectual courage is a crime, that
cowardice is a virtue, that a certain belief is necessary to
secure salvation, that to carry a cross in this world will give us
a palm in the next, and that we must allow some priest to be
the pilot of our souls.

Until every soul is freely permitted to investigate every
book, and creed, and dogma for itself, the world cannot be
free.

Mankind will be enslaved until there is mental grandeur
enough to allow each man to have his thought and say. This
earth will be a paradise when men can, upon all these
questions differ, and yet grasp each other's hands as friends.
It is amazing to me that a difference of opinion upon subjects
that we know nothing with certainty about, should make us
hate, persecute, and despise each other. Why a difference of
opinion upon predestination, or the Trinity, should make
people imprison and burn each other seems beyond the
comprehension of man; and yet in all countries where
Christians have existed, they have destroyed each other to the

exact extent of their power. Why should a believer in God hate an atheist? Surely the atheist has not injured God, and surely he is human, capable of joy and pain, and entitled to all the rights of man. Would it not be far better to treat this atheist, at least, as well as he treats us?

Christians tell me that they love their enemies, and yet all I ask is—not that they love their enemies, not that they love their friends even, but that they treat those who differ from them, with simple fairness. We do not wish to be forgiven, but we wish Christians to so act that we will not have to forgive them.

If all will admit that all have an equal right to think, then the question is forever solved; but as long as organized and powerful churches, pretending to hold the keys of heaven and hell, denounce every person as an outcast and criminal who thinks for himself and denies their authority, the world will be filled with hatred and suffering. ...

That which has happened in most countries has happened in ours. When a religion is founded, the educated, the powerful—that is to say, the priests and nobles, tell the ignorant and superstitious—that is to say, the people, that the religion of their country was given to their fathers by God himself; that it is the only true religion; that all others were conceived in falsehood and brought forth in fraud, and that all who believe in the true religion will be happy forever, while all others will burn in hell.

For the purpose of governing the people, that is to say, for the purpose of being supported by the people, the priests and nobles declare this religion to be sacred, and that whoever adds to, or takes away from it, will be burned here by man, and hereafter by God. The result of this is, that the priests and nobles will not allow the people to change; and when, after a time, the priests, having intellectually advanced, wish to take a step in the direction of progress, the people will not allow them to change. At first, the rabble are enslaved by the priests, and afterwards the rabble become the masters.

One of the first things I wish to do, is to free the orthodox clergy. I am a great friend of theirs, and in spite of all they may say against me, I am going to do them a great and lasting service.

Upon their necks are visible the marks of the collar, and upon their backs those of the lash. They are not allowed to read and think for themselves. They are taught like parrots, and the best are those who repeat, with the fewest mistakes, the sentences they have been taught. They sit like owls upon some dead limb of the tree of knowledge, and hoot the same old hoots that have been hooted for eighteen hundred years. Their congregations are not grand enough, nor sufficiently civilized, to be willing that the poor preachers shall think for themselves. They are not employed for that purpose. Investigation is regarded as a dangerous experiment, and the ministers are warned that none of that kind of work will be tolerated. They are notified to stand by the old creed, and to avoid all original thought, as a moral pestilence. Every minister is employed like an attorney—either for plaintiff or defendant,—and he is expected to be true to his client. If he changes his mind, he is regarded as a deserter, and denounced, hated, and slandered accordingly. Every orthodox clergyman agrees not to change. He contracts not to find new facts, and makes a bargain that he will deny them if he does. Such is the position of a Protestant minister in this nineteenth century. His condition excites my pity; and to better it, I am going to do what little I can.

Some of the clergy have the independence to break away, and the intellect to maintain themselves as free men, but the most are compelled to submit to the dictation of the orthodox, and the dead. They are not employed to give their thoughts, but simply to repeat the ideas of others. They are not expected to give even the doubts that may suggest themselves, but are required to walk in the narrow, verdureless path trodden by the ignorance of the past. The forests and fields on either side are nothing to them. They must not even look at the purple hills, nor pause to hear the babble of the brooks. They must remain in the dusty road where the guide-boards are. They must confine themselves to the "fall of man," "the expulsion from the garden," the "scheme of salvation," the "second birth," the atonement, the happiness of the redeemed, and the misery of the lost. They must be careful not to express any new ideas upon these great questions. It is much safer for them to quote from the works of the dead. The more vividly they describe the sufferings of the unregenerate, of those who attended theaters and balls, and drank wine in summer gardens on the Sabbath-day, and laughed at priests, the better ministers they are supposed to be.

They must show that misery fits the good for heaven, while happiness prepares the bad for hell; that the wicked get all their good things in this life, and the good all their evil; that in this world God punishes the people he loves, and in the next, the ones he hates; that happiness makes us bad here, but not in heaven; that pain makes us good here, but not in hell. No matter how absurd these things may appear to the carnal mind, they must be preached and they must he believed. If they were reasonable, there would be no virtue in believing. Even the publicans and sinners believe reasonable things. To believe without evidence, or in spite of it, is accounted as righteousness to the sincere and humble Christian.

The ministers are in duty bound to denounce all intellectual pride, and show that we are never quite so dear to God as when we admit that we are poor, corrupt and idiotic worms; that we never should have been born; that we ought to be damned without the least delay; that we are so infamous that we like to enjoy ourselves; that we love our wives and children better than our God; that we are generous only because we are vile; that we are honest from the meanest motives, and that sometimes we have fallen so low that we have had doubts about the inspiration of the Jewish Scriptures. ... They are expected to point out the dangers of freedom, the safety of implicit obedience, and to show the wickedness of philosophy, the goodness of faith, the immorality of science and the purity of ignorance.

Now and then a few pious people discover some young man of a religious turn of mind and a consumptive habit of holy, not quite sickly enough to die, nor healthy enough to be wicked. The idea occurs to them that he would make a good orthodox minister. They take up a contribution, and send the young man to some theological school where he can be taught to repeat a creed and despise reason. Should it turn out that the young man had some mind of his own, and, after graduating, should change his opinions and preach a different doctrine from that taught in the school, every man who contributed a dollar towards his education would feel that he had been robbed, and would denounce him as a dishonest and ungrateful wretch. ...

They have, in Massachusetts, at a place called Andover, a kind of minister factory, where each professor takes an oath once in five years—that time being considered the life of an oath—that he has not, during the last five years, and will not, during the next five years, intellectually advance. There is probably no oath that they could easier keep. Probably, since the foundation stone of that institution was laid there has not been a single case of perjury. The old creed is still taught. They still insist that God is infinitely wise, powerful and good, and that all men are totally depraved. They insist that the best man God ever made, deserved to he damned the moment he was finished. Andover puts its brand upon every minister it turns out, the same as Sheffield and Birmingham brand their wares, and all who see the brand know exactly what the minister believes, the books he has read, the arguments he relies on, and just what he intellectually is. They know just what he can be depended on to preach, and that he will continue to shrink and shrivel, and grow solemnly stupid day by day until he reaches the Andover of the grave and becomes truly orthodox forever.

I have not singled out the Andover factory because it is worse than the others. They are all about the same. The professors, for the most part, are ministers who failed in the pulpit and were retired to the seminary on account of their deficiency in reason and their excess of faith. As a rule, they know nothing of this world, and far less of the next; but they have the power of stating the most absurd propositions with faces solemn an stupidity touched by fear. ...

The clergy, however, will continue to answer them in the old way, until their congregations are good enough to set them free. ...

Until the clergy are free they cannot be intellectually honest. We can never tell what they really believe until they know that they can safely speak. They console themselves now by a secret resolution to be as liberal as they dare, with the hope that they can finally educate their congregations to the point of allowing them to think a little for themselves. They hardly know what they ought to do. The best part of their lives has been wasted in studying subjects of no possible value. Most of them are married, have families, and know but one way of making their living. Some of them say that if they do not preach these foolish dogmas, others will, and that they may through fear, after all, restrain mankind. Besides, they hate publicly to admit that they are mistaken, that the whole thing is a delusion, that the "scheme of salvation" is absurd, and that the Bible is no better than some other books, and worse than most.

You can hardly expect a bishop to leave his palace, or the pope to vacate the Vatican. As long as people want popes, plenty of hypocrites will be found to take the place. And as long as labor fatigues, there will be found a good many men willing to preach once a week, if other folks will work and give them bread. In other words, while the demand lasts, the supply will never fail.

THE POLITICIANS

There are so many societies, so many churches, so many isms, that it is almost impossible for an independent man to succeed in a political career. Candidates are forced to pretend that they are Catholics with Protestant proclivities, or Christians with liberal tendencies, or temperance men who now and then take a glass of wine, or, that although not members of any church their wives are, and that they subscribe liberally to all. The result of all this is that we reward hypocrisy and elect men entirely destitute of real principle; and this will never change until the people become grand enough to allow each other to do their own thinking.

Our Government should be entirely and purely secular. The religious views of a candidate should be kept entirely out of sight. He should not be compelled to give his opinion as to the inspiration of the Bible, the propriety of infant baptism, or the immaculate conception. All these things are private and personal.

MAN AND WOMAN.
...

We know that our opinions depend, to a great degree, upon our surroundings—upon race, country, and education. We are all the result of numberless conditions, and inherit vices and virtues, truths and prejudices. If we had been born in England, surrounded by wealth and clothed with power, most of us would have been Episcopalians, and believed in church and state. We should have insisted that the people needed a religion, and that not having intellect enough to provide one for themselves, it was our duty to make one for them, and then compel them to support it. We should have believed it indecent to officiate in a pulpit without wearing a gown, and that prayers should be read from a book. Had we belonged to the lower classes, we might have been dissenters and protested against the mummeries of the High Church. Had we been born in Turkey, most of us would have been Mohammedans [Muslims] and believed in the inspiration of the Koran. We should have believed that Mohammed actually visited heaven and became acquainted with an angel by the name of Gabriel, who was so broad between the eyes that it required three hundred days for a very smart camel to travel the distance. If some man had denied this story we should probably have denounced him as a dangerous person, one who was endeavoring to undermine the foundations of society, and to destroy all distinction between virtue and vice. We should have said to him, "What do you propose to give us in place of that angel? We cannot afford to give up an angel of that size for nothing." We would have insisted that the best and wisest men believed the Koran. We would have quoted from the works and letters of philosophers, generals and sultans, to show that the Koran was the best of books, and that Turkey was indebted to that book and to that alone for its greatness and prosperity. We would have asked that man whether he knew more than all the great minds of his country, whether he was so much wiser than his fathers? We would have pointed out to him the fact that thousands had been consoled in the hour of death by passages from the Koran; that they had died with glazed eyes brightened by visions of the heavenly harem, and gladly left this world of grief and tears. We would have regarded Christians as the vilest of men, and on all occasions would have repeated "There is but one God, and Mohammed is his prophet!"

So, if we had been born in India, we should in all probability have believed in the religion of that country. We should have regarded the old records as true and sacred, and looked upon a wandering priest as better than the men from whom he begged, and by whose labor he lived. We should have believed in a god with three heads instead of three gods with one head, as we do now.

Now and then some one says that the religion of his father and mother is good enough for him, and wonders why anybody should desire a better. Surely we are not bound to follow our parents in religion any more than in politics, science or art. ... If we are, in any way, bound by the belief of our fathers, the doctrine will hold good back to the first people who had a religion; and if this doctrine is true, we ought now to be believers in that first religion. In other words, we would all be barbarians. You cannot show real respect to your parents by perpetuating their errors. ...

We must remember that this "ancestor" argument is as old at least as the second generation of men, that it has served no purpose except to enslave mankind, and results mostly from the fact that acquiescence is easier than investigation. This argument pushed to its logical conclusion, would prevent the advance of all people whose parents were not Freethinkers.

It is hard for many people to give up the religion in which they were born; to admit that their fathers were utterly mistaken, and that the sacred records of their country are but collections of myths and fables.

But when we look for a moment at the world, we find that each nation has its "sacred records"—its religion, and its ideas of worship. Certainly all cannot be right; and as it would require a lifetime to investigate the claims of these various systems, it is hardly fair to damn a man forever, simply because he happens to believe the wrong one. ...

Nearly all these religions are intensely selfish. Each one was made by some contemptible little nation that regarded itself as of almost infinite importance, and looked upon the other nations as beneath the notice of their god. In all these countries it was a crime to deny the sacred records, to laugh at the priests, to speak disrespectfully of the gods, to fail to divide your substance with the lazy hypocrites who managed your affairs in the next world upon condition that you would support them in this. In the olden time these theological people who quartered themselves upon the honest and industrious, were called soothsayers, seers, charmers, prophets, enchanters, sorcerers, wizards, astrologers, and impostors, but now, they are known as clergymen.

We are no exception to the general rule, and consequently have our sacred books as well as the rest. Of course, it is claimed by many of our people that our books are the only true ones, the only ones that the real God ever wrote, or had anything whatever to do with. They insist that all other sacred books were written by hypocrites and impostors; that the Jews were the only people that God ever had any personal intercourse with, and that all other prophets and seers were inspired only by impudence and mendacity.

True, it seems somewhat strange that God should have chosen a barbarous and unknown people who had little or nothing to do with the other nations of the earth, as his messengers to the rest of mankind.

It is not easy to … perceive why, if a revelation was necessary for all, it was made only to a few. Of course, I know that it is extremely wicked to suggest these thoughts, and that ignorance is the only armor that can effectually protect you from the wrath of God. …

Whoever reads our sacred book is compelled to believe it or suffer forever the torments of the lost. We are told that we have the privilege of examining it for ourselves; but this privilege is only extended to us on the condition that we believe it whether it appears reasonable or not. We may disagree with others as much as we please upon the meaning of all passages in the Bible, but we must not deny the truth of a single word. We must believe that the book is inspired. If we obey its every precept without believing in its inspiration we will be damned just as certainly as though we disobeyed its every word. We have no right to weigh it in the scales of reason—to test it by the laws of nature, or the facts of observation and experience. To do this, we are told, is to put ourselves above the word of God, and sit in judgment on the works of our creator. ...

For my part, I cannot admit that belief is a voluntary thing. It seems to me that evidence, even in spite of ourselves, will have its weight, and that whatever our wish may be, we are compelled to stand with fairness by the scales, and give the exact result. It will not do to say that we reject the Bible because we are wicked. Our wickedness must be ascertained not from our belief but from our acts. ...

The real oppressor, enslaver and corrupter of the people is the Bible. That book is the chain that binds, the dungeon that holds the clergy. That book spreads the pall of superstition over the colleges and schools. That book puts out the eyes of science, and makes honest investigation a crime. That book unmans the politician and degrades the people.

That book fills the world with bigotry, hypocrisy and fear. It plays the same part in our country that has been played by "sacred records" in all the nations of the world.

A little while ago I saw one of the Bibles of the Middle Ages. It was about two feet in length, and one and a half in width. It had immense oaken covers, with hasps, and clasps, and hinges large enough almost for the doors of a penitentiary. It was covered with pictures of winged angels and aureoled saints. In my imagination I saw this book carried to the cathedral altar in solemn pomp—heard the chant of robed and kneeling priests, felt the strange tremor of the organ's peal; saw the colored light streaming through windows stained and touched by blood and flame—the swinging censer with its perfumed incense rising to the mighty roof, dim with height and rich with legend carved in stone, while on the walls was hung, written in light, and shade, and all the colors that can tell of joy and tears, the pictured history of the martyred Christ. The people fell upon their knees. The book was opened, and the priest read the messages from God to man. To the multitude, the book itself was evidence enough that it was not the work of human hands. How could those little marks and lines and dots contain, like tombs, the thoughts of men, and how could they, touched by a ray of light from human eyes, give up their dead? How could these characters span the vast chasm dividing the present from the past, and make it possible for the living still to hear the voices of the dead?

THE PENTATEUCH.

The first five books in our Bible are known as the Pentateuch. For a long time it was supposed that Moses was the author, and among the ignorant the supposition still prevails. As a matter of fact, it seems to be well settled that Moses had nothing to do with these books, and that they were not written until he had been dust and ashes for hundreds of years. But, as all the churches still insist that he was the author, that he wrote even an account of his own death and burial, let us speak of him as though these books were in fact written by him. As the Christians maintain that God was the real author, it makes but little difference whom he employed as his pen, or clerk.

Nearly all authors of sacred books have given an account of the creation of the universe, the origin of matter, and the destiny of the human race. Nearly all have pointed out the obligation that man is under to his creator for having placed him upon the earth, and allowed him to live and suffer, and have taught that nothing short of the most abject worship could possibly compensate God for his trouble and labor suffered and done for the good of man. They have nearly all insisted that we should thank God for all that is good in life but they have not all informed us as to whom we should hold responsible for the evils we endure.

Moses differed from most of the makers of sacred books by his failure to say anything of a future life, by failing to promise heaven, and to threaten hell. Upon the subject of a future state, there is not one word in the Pentateuch. Probably at that early day God did not deem it important to make a revelation as to the eternal destiny of man. He seems to have thought that he could control the Jews, at least, by rewards and punishments in this world, and so he kept the frightful realities of eternal joy and torment a profound secret from the people of his choice. He thought it far more important to tell the Jews their origin than to enlighten them as to their destiny.

We must remember that every tribe and nation has some way in which the more striking phenomena of nature are accounted for. These accounts are handed down by tradition, changed by numberless narrators as intelligence increases, or to account for newly discovered facts, or for the purpose of satisfying the appetite for the marvelous.

The way in which a tribe or nation accounts for day and night, the change of seasons, the fall of snow and rain, the flight of birds, the origin of the rainbow, the peculiarities of animals, the dreams of sleep, the visions of the insane, the existence of earthquakes, volcanoes, storms, lightning and the thousand things that attract the attention and excite the wonder, fear or admiration of mankind, may be called the philosophy of that tribe or nation. And as all phenomena are, by savage and barbaric man accounted for as the action of intelligent beings for the accomplishment of certain objects, and as these beings were supposed to have the power to assist or injure man, certain things were supposed necessary for man to do in order to gain the assistance, and avoid the anger of these gods. Out of this belief grew certain ceremonies, and these ceremonies united with the belief, formed religion; and consequently every religion has for its foundation a misconception of the cause of phenomena.

All worship is necessarily based upon the belief that some being exists who can, if he will, change the natural order of events. The savage prays to a stone that he calls a god, while the Christian prays to a god that he calls a spirit, and the prayers of both are equally useful. The savage and the Christian put behind the Universe an intelligent cause, and this cause whether represented by one god or many, has been, in all ages, the object of all worship. To carry a fetich, to utter a prayer, to count beads, to abstain from food, to sacrifice a lamb, a child or an enemy, are simply different ways by which the accomplishment of the same object is sought, and are all the offspring of the same error.

Many systems of religion must have existed many ages before the art of writing was discovered, and must have passed through many changes before the stories, miracles, histories, prophecies and mistakes became fixed and petrified in written words. After that, change was possible only by giving new meanings to old words, a process rendered necessary by the continual acquisition of facts somewhat inconsistent with a literal interpretation of the "sacred records." In this way an honest faith often prolongs its life by dishonest methods; and in this way the Christians of today are trying to harmonize the Mosaic account of creation with the theories and discoveries of modern science.

Admitting that Moses was the author of the Pentateuch,

or that he gave to the Jews a religion, the question arises as to where he obtained his information. We are told by the theologians that he received his knowledge from God, and that every word he wrote was and is the exact truth. It is admitted at the same time that he was an adopted son of Pharaoh's daughter, and enjoyed the rank and privilege of a prince. Under such circumstances, he must have been well acquainted with the literature, philosophy and religion of the Egyptians, and must have known what they believed and taught as to the creation of the world.

Now, if the account of the origin of this earth as given by Moses is substantially like that given by the Egyptians, then we must conclude that he learned it from them. Should we imagine that he was divinely inspired because he gave to the Jews what the Egyptians had given him?

The Egyptian priests taught first, that a god created the "original matter" leaving it in a state of chaos; second, that a god molded it into from; third, that the breath of a god moved upon the face of the deep; fourth, that a god created simply by saying "Let it be;" fifth, that a god created light before the sun existed.

...Moses received from the Egyptians the principal parts of his narrative, making such changes and additions as were necessary to satisfy the peculiar superstitions of his own people.

...

[BELIEVE, AND OBEY!]

In order to increase our respect for the Bible, it became necessary for the priests to exalt and extol that book, and at the same time to decry and belittle the reasoning powers of man. The whole power of the pulpit has been used for hundreds of years to destroy the confidence of man in himself—to induce him to distrust his own powers of thought, to believe that he was wholly unable to decide any question for himself and that all human virtue consists in faith and obedience.

The church has said, "Believe, and obey! If you reason, you will become an unbeliever, and unbelievers will be lost. If you disobey, you will do so through vain pride and curiosity, and will, like Adam and Eve, be thrust from Paradise forever."

[MANKIND]

… [In the Bible,] how were Adam and Eve created? In one account they are created male and female, and apparently at the same time. In the next account, Adam is created first, and Eve a long time afterwards, and from a part of the man.

… If the Mosaic account is true, we know how long man has been upon this earth. If that account can be relied on, the first man was made about five thousand eight hundred and eighty-three years ago. Sixteen hundred and fifty-six years after the making of the first man, the inhabitants of the world, with the exception of eight people, were destroyed by a flood. This flood occurred only about four thousand two hundred and twenty-seven years ago. If this account is correct, at that time, only one kind of men existed. Noah and his family were certainly of the same blood. It therefore follows that all the differences we see between the various races of men have been caused in about four thousand years. If the account of the deluge is true, then since that event all the ancient kingdoms of the earth were founded, and their inhabitants passed through all the stages of savage, nomadic, barbaric and semi-civilized life; through the epochs of Stone, Bronze and Iron; established commerce, cultivated the arts, built cities, filled them with palaces and temples, invented writing, produced a literature and slowly fell to shapeless ruin. We must believe that all this has happened within a period of four thousand years. ...

If we know anything, we know that magnificent statues were made in Egypt four thousand years before our era—that is to say, about six thousand years ago. There was at the World's Exposition, in the Egyptian department, a statue of king Cephren, known to have been chiseled more than six thousand years ago. In other words, if the Mosaic account must be believed, this statue was made before the world. We also know, if we know anything, that men lived in Europe with the hairy mammoth, the cave bear, the rhinoceros, and the hyena. Among the bones of these animals have been found the stone hatchets and flint arrows of our ancestors. In the caves where they lived have been discovered the remains of these animals that had been conquered, killed and devoured as food, hundreds of thousands of years ago.

If these facts are true, Moses was mistaken. For my part, I have infinitely more confidence in the discoveries of today, than in the records of a barbarous people. It will not now do to say that man has existed upon this earth for only about six thousand years. One can hardly compute in his imagination the time necessary for man to emerge from the barbarous state, naked and helpless, surrounded by animals far more powerful than he, to progress and finally create the civilizations of India, Egypt and Athens.

[TWO CREATION ACCOUNTS]

It must not be forgotten that there are two accounts of the creation in Genesis. The first account stops with the third verse of the second chapter. The chapters have been improperly divided. In the original Hebrew the Pentateuch was neither divided into chapters nor verses. There was not even any system of punctuation. It was written wholly with consonants, without vowels, and without any marks, dots, or lines to indicate them.

These accounts are materially different, and both cannot be true. Let us see wherein they differ.

...

ORDER OF CREATION IN THE FIRST ACCOUNT:

   1.   The heaven and the earth, and light were made.

   2. The firmament was constructed and the waters divided.

   3. The waters gathered into seas—and then came dry land, grass, herbs and fruit trees.

   4. The sun and moon. He made the stars also.

   5. Fishes, fowls, and great whales.

   6. Beasts, cattle, every creeping thing, man and woman.

ORDER OF CREATION IN THE SECOND ACCOUNT:

   1. The heavens and the earth.

   2. A mist went up from the earth, and watered the whole face of the ground.

   3. Created a man out of dust, by the name of Adam.

   4. Planted a garden eastward in Eden, and put the man in it.

   5. Created the beasts and fowls.

   6. Created a woman out of one of the man's ribs.

In the second account, man was made before the beasts and fowls. If this is true, the first account is false. ...

[THE FLOOD]

"And it came to pass, when men began to multiply on the face of the earth, and daughters were born unto them.

"That the sons of God saw the daughters of men that they

were fair; and they took them wives of all which they chose.

"And the Lord said, My spirit shall not always strive with man, for that he also is flesh; yet his days shall be an hundred and twenty years.

"There were giants in the earth in those days; and also after that when the sons of God came in unto the daughters of men, and they bare children to them, the same became mighty men which were of old, men of renown.

"And God saw that the wickedness of man was great in the earth, and that every imagination of the thoughts of his heart was only evil continually.

"And it repented the Lord that he had made man on the earth, and it grieved him at his heart.

"And the Lord said, I will destroy man whom I have created from the face of the earth; both man and beast, and the creeping thing, and the fowls of the air; for it repenteth me that I have made them."

From this account it seems that driving Adam and Eve out of Eden did not have the effect to improve them or their children. On the contrary, the world grew worse and worse. They were under the immediate control and government of God, and he from time to time made known his will; but in spite of this, man continued to increase in crime.

Nothing in particular seems to have been done. Not a school was established. There was no written language. There was not a Bible in the world. The "scheme of salvation" was kept a profound secret. The five points of Calvinism had not been taught. Sunday schools had not been opened. In short, nothing had been done for the reformation of the world. God did not even keep his own sons at home, but allowed them to leave their abode in the firmament, and make love to the daughters of men. As a result of this, the world was filled with wickedness and giants to such an extent that God regretted "that he had made man on the earth, and it grieved him at his heart."

Of course God knew when he made man, that he would afterwards regret it. He knew that the people would grow worse and worse until destruction would be the only remedy. He knew that he would have to kill all except Noah and his family, and it is hard to see why he did not make Noah and his family in the first place, and leave Adam and Eve in the original dust. He knew that they would be tempted, that he would have to drive them out of the garden to keep them from eating of the tree of life; that the whole thing would be a failure; that Satan would defeat his plan; that he could not reform the people; that his own sons would corrupt them, and that at last he would have to drown them all except Noah and his family. Why was the Garden of Eden planted? Why was the experiment made? Why were Adam and Eve exposed to the seductive arts of the serpent? Why did God wait until the cool of the day before looking after his children? Why was he not on hand in the morning? Why did he fill the world with his own children, knowing that he would have to destroy them? And why does this same God tell me how to raise my children when he had to drown his?

It is a little curious that when God wished to reform the

ante-diluvian world he said nothing about hell; that he had no revivals, no camp-meetings, no tracts, no outpourings of the Holy Ghost, no baptisms, no noon prayer meetings, and never mentioned the great doctrine of salvation by faith. If the orthodox creeds of the world are true, all those people want to hell without ever having heard that such a place existed. If eternal torment is a fact, surely these miserable wretches ought to have been warned. They were threatened only with water when they were in fact doomed to eternal fire!

Is it not strange that God said nothing to Adam and Eve about a future life; that he should have kept these "infinite verities" to himself and allowed millions to live and die without the hope of heaven, or the fear of hell?"

It may be that hell was not made at that time. In the six days of creation nothing is said about the construction of a bottomless pit, and the serpent himself did not make his appearance until after the creation of man and woman. Perhaps he was made on the first Sunday, and from that fact came, it may be, the old couplet; "And Satan still some mischief finds for idle hands to do."

The sacred historian failed also to tell us when the cherubim and the flaming sword were made, and said nothing about two of the persons composing the Trinity. It certainly would have been an easy thing to enlighten Adam and his immediate descendants. The world was then only about fifteen hundred and thirty-six years old, and only about three or four generations of men had lived. Adam had been dead only about six hundred and six years, and some of his grandchildren must, at that time, have been alive and well.

It is hard to see why God did not civilize these people. He certainly had the power to use, and the wisdom, to devise the proper means. What right has a god to fill a world with fiends? Can there be goodness in this? Why should he make experiments that he knows must fail? Is there wisdom in this? And what right has a man to charge an infinite being with wickedness and folly?

According to Moses, God made up his mind not only to destroy the people, but the beasts and the creeping things, and the fowls of the air. What had creeping things, and the fowls of the air done? What had the beasts, and the birds done to excite the anger of God? Why did he repent having made them? Will some Christian give us an explanation of this matter? No good man will inflict unnecessary pain upon a beast; how then can we worship a god who cares nothing for the agonies of the dumb creatures that he made?

Why did he make animals that he knew he would destroy? Does God delight in causing pain? He had the power to make the beasts, and fowls, and creeping things in his own good time and way, and it is to be presumed that he made them according to his wish. Why should he destroy them? They had committed no sin. They had eaten no forbidden fruit, made no aprons, nor tried to reach the tree of life. Yet this god, in blind unreasoning wrath destroyed "all flesh wherein was the breath of life, and every living thing beneath the sky, and every substance wherein was life that he had made."

Jehovah having made up his mind to drown the world, told Noah to make an Ark of gopher wood three hundred cubits long, fifty cubits wide and thirty cubits high. A cubit is twenty-two inches; so that the ark was five hundred and fifty feet long, ninety one feet and eight inches wide and fifty-five feet high. This ark was divided into three stories, and had on top, one window twenty-two inches square. Ventilation must have been one of Jehovah's hobbies. Think of a ship larger than the Great Eastern with only one window, and that but twenty two inches square!

The ark also had one door set in the side thereof that shut from the outside. As soon as this ship was finished, and properly victualed, Noah received seven days notice to get the animals in the ark.

It is claimed by some of the scientific theologians that the flood was partial, that the waters covered only a small portion of the world, and that consequently only a few animals were in the ark. It is impossible to conceive of language that can more clearly convey the idea of a universal flood than that found in the inspired account. If the flood was only partial, why did God say he would "destroy all flesh wherein is the breath of life from under heaven, and that every thing that is in the earth shall die"? Why did he say "I will destroy man whom I have created from the face of the earth, both man and beast, and the creeping thing and the fowls of the air"? Why did he say "And every living substance that I have made will I destroy from off the face of the earth"? Would a partial, local flood have fulfilled these threats?

Nothing can be clearer than that the writer of this account intended to convey, and did convey the idea that the flood was universal. ...

... [And] how many beasts, fowls and creeping things did Noah take into the ark?

There are now known and classified at least twelve thousand five hundred species of birds. There are still vast territories in China, South America, and Africa unknown to the ornithologist.

Of the birds, Noah took fourteen of each species, according to the 3d verse of the 7th chapter, "Of fowls also of the air by sevens; the male and the female," making a total of 175,000 birds. ...

There are at least sixteen hundred and fifty-eight kinds of beasts. Let us suppose that twenty-five of these are clean. Of the clean, fourteen of each kind—seven of each sex—were taken. These amount to 350. Of the unclean—two of each kind, amounting to 3,266. There are some six hundred and fifty species of reptiles. Two of each kind amount to 1,300. And lastly, there are of insects including the creeping things, at least one million species, so that Noah and his folks had to get of these into the ark about 2,000,000.

Animalcule have not been taken into consideration. There are probably many hundreds of thousands of species; many of them invisible; and yet Noah had to pick them out by pairs. Very few people have any just conception of the trouble Noah had.

We know that there are many animals on this continent

not found in the Old world. These must have been carried from here to the ark, and then brought back afterwards. Were the peccary, armadillo, ant-eater, sloth, agouti, vampire-bat, marmoset, howling and prehensile-tailed monkey, the raccoon and muskrat carried by the angels from America to Asia? How did they get there? Did the polar bear leave his field of ice and journey toward the tropics? How did he know where the ark was? Did the kangaroo swim or jump from Australia to Asia? Did the giraffe, hippopotamus, antelope and orangoutang journey from Africa in search of the ark? Can absurdities go farther than this?

What had these animals to eat while on the journey? What did they eat while in the ark? What did they drink? ...

Noah had to take in his ark fresh water for all his beasts, birds and living things. He had to take the proper food for all. How long was he in the ark? Three hundred and seventy-seven days!

Think of the food necessary for the monsters of the ante-diluvian world!

Eight persons did all the work. They attended to the wants of 175,000 birds, 3,616 beasts, 1,300 reptiles, and 2,000,000 insects, saying nothing of countless animalcule. ...

How could eight persons have distributed this food, even if the ark had been large enough to hold it? How was the ark kept clean? We know how it was ventilated; but what was done with the filth? How were the animals watered? How were some portions of the ark heated for animals from the tropics, and others kept cool for the polar bears? How did the animals get back to their respective countries? Some had to creep back about six thousand miles, and they could only go a few feet a day. Some of the creeping things must have started for the ark just as soon as they were made, and kept up a steady jog for sixteen hundred years. Think of a couple of the slowest snails leaving a point opposite the ark and starting for the plains of Shinar, a distance of twelve thousand miles.

Going at the rate of a mile a month, it would take them a thousand years. How did they get there? Polar bears must have gone several thousand miles, and so sudden a change in climate must have been exceedingly trying upon their health. How did they know the way to go? Of course, all the polar bears did not go. Only two were required. Who selected these? ...

Volumes might be written upon the infinite absurdity of this most incredible, wicked and foolish of all the fables contained in that repository of the impossible, called the Bible. To me it is a matter of amazement, that it ever was for a moment believed by any intelligent human being.

Dr. Adam Clarke says that "the animals were brought to the ark by the power of God, and their enmities were so removed or suspended, that the lion could dwell peaceably with the lamb, and the wolf sleep happily by the side of the kid. There is no positive evidence that animal food was ever used before the flood. Noah had the first grant of this kind."

Dr. Scott remarks, "There seems to have been a very extraordinary miracle, perhaps by the ministration of angels, in bringing two of every species to Noah, and rendering them submissive, and peaceful with each other. Yet it seems not to have made any impression upon the hardened spectators. The suspension of the ferocity of the savage beasts during their continuance in the ark is generally considered as an apt figure of the change that takes place in the disposition of sinners when they enter the true church of Christ." ...

...

[ABRAHAM]

...

God made a great number of promises to Abraham, but few of them were ever kept. He agreed to make him the father of a great nation, but he did not. He solemnly promised to give him a great country, including all the land between the river of Egypt and the Euphrates, but he did not.

"INSPIRED" SLAVERY

Perhaps the bible was inspired upon the subject of human slavery. Is there, in the civilized world, today, a clergyman who believes in the divinity of slavery? Does the bible teach man to enslave his brother? If it does, is it not blasphemous to say that it is inspired of God? If you find the institution of slavery upheld in a book said to have been written by God, what would you expect to find in a book inspired by the devil? Would you expect to find that book in favor of liberty?

Modern Christians, ashamed of the God of the Old

Testament, endeavor now to show that slavery was neither commanded nor opposed by Jehovah. Nothing can be plainer than the following passages from the twenty-fifth chapter of Leviticus: "Moreover of the children of the strangers that do sojourn among you, of them shall ye buy, and of their families that are with you, which they begat in your land: and they shall be your possession. And ye shall take them as an inheritance for your children after you, to inherit them for a possession, they shall be your bond-men forever. Both thy bond-men, and thy bond-maids, which thou shalt have, shall be of the heathen that are round about you; of them shall ye buy bond-men, and bond-maids."

Can we believe in this, the Nineteenth Century, that these infamous passages were inspired by God? that God approved not only of human slavery, but instructed his chosen people to buy the women, children and babies of the heathen round about them? If it was right for the Hebrews to buy, it was also right for the heathen to sell. This God, by commanding the Hebrews to buy, approved of the selling of sons and daughters. The Canaanite who, tempted by gold, lured by avarice, sold from the arms of his wife the dimpled baby, simply made it possible for the Hebrews to obey the orders of their God. If God is the author of the bible, the reading of these passages ought to cover his cheeks with shame. Ask the Christian world today, was it right for heathen to sell their children? Was it right for God not only to uphold, but to command the most revengeful fiend, the most malicious vagrant in the gloom of hell, sink to a lower moral depth than this?

According to this God, his chosen people were not only commanded to buy of the heathen round about them, but were also permitted to buy each other for a term of years. The law governing the purchase of Jews is laid down in the twenty-first chapter of Exodus: "If thou buy a Hebrew servant, six years shall he serve and in the seventh he shall go out free for nothing. If he came in by himself, he shall go out by himself: If he were married then his wife shall go out with him. If his master have given him a wife, and she have borne him sons or daughters, the wife and her children shall be her masters, and he shall go out by himself. And if the servant shall plainly say, I love my master, my wife, and my children; I will not go out free. Then his master shall bring him unto the judges; he shall also bring him to the door, or unto the door-post: and his master shall bore his ear through with an awl: and he shall serve him forever."

Do you believe that God was the author of this infamous law? Do you believe that the loving father of us all, turned the dimpled arms of babes into manacles of iron? Do you believe that he baited the dungeon of servitude with wife and child? ...

The heathen are not spoken of as human beings. Their rights are never mentioned. They were the rightful food of the sword, and their bodies were made for stripes and chains.

In the same chapter of the same inspired book, we are told that, "if a man smite his servant, or his maid, with a rod, and he dies under his hand, he shall be surely punished.

Notwithstanding, if he continue a day or two, he shall not be punished, for he is his money."

Must we believe that God called some of his children the money of others? Can we believe that God made lashes upon the naked back, a legal tender for labor performed? Must we regard the auction block as an altar? Were blood hounds apostles? Was the slave-pen a temple? Were the stealers and whippers of babies and women the justified children of God?

It is now contended that while the Old Testament is touched with the barbarism of its time, that the New Testament is morally perfect, and that on its pages can be found no blot or stain. As a matter of fact, the New Testament is more decidedly in favor of human slavery than the old.

For my part, I never will, I never can, worship a God who upholds the institution of slavery. ...

"INSPIRED" WAR

If the Bible be true, God commanded his chosen people to destroy men simply for the crime of defending their native land. They were not allowed to spare trembling and white-haired age, nor dimpled babes clasped in the mothers' arms. They were ordered to kill women, and to pierce, with the sword of war, the unborn child. "Our heavenly Father" commanded the Hebrews to kill the men and women, the fathers, sons and brothers, but to preserve the girls alive.

Why were not the maidens also killed? Why were they spared? Read the thirty-first chapter of Numbers, and you will find that the maidens were given to the soldiers and the priests. Is there, in all the history of war, a more infamous thing than this? Is it possible that God permitted the violets of modesty, that grow and shed their perfume in the maiden's heart, to be trampled beneath the brutal feet of lust? If this was the order of God, what, under the same circumstances, would have been the command of a devil? When, in this age of the world, a woman, a wife, a mother, reads this record, she should, with scorn and loathing, throw the book away. A general, who now should make such an order, giving over to massacre and rapine a conquered people, would be held in execration by the whole civilized world. Yet, if the bible be true, the supreme and infinite God was once a savage.

A little while ago, out upon the western plains, in a little path leading to a cabin, were found the bodies of two children and their mother. Her breast was filled with wounds received in the defence of her darlings. They had been murdered by the savages. Suppose when looking at their lifeless forms, some one had said, "This was done by the command of God!" In Canaan there were countless scenes like this. There was no pity in inspired war. God raised the black flag, and commanded his soldiers to kill even the smiling infant in its mother's arms. Who is the blasphemer; the man who denies the existence of God, or he who covers the robes of the Infinite with innocent blood?

We are told in the Pentateuch, that God, the father of us

all, gave thousands of maidens, after having killed their fathers, their mothers, and their brothers, to satisfy the brutal lusts of savage men. …

"INSPIRED" RELIGIOUS LIBERTY

In the thirteenth chapter of Deuteronomy, we have the ideas of God as to mental freedom: "If thy brother, the son of thy mother, or thy son, or the wife of thy bosom, or thy friend which is as thine own soul, entice thee secretly, saying, Let us go and serve other gods, which thou hast not known, thou nor thy fathers; namely of the gods of the people which are around about you, nigh unto thee, or far off from thee, from the one end of the earth even unto the other end of the earth, Thou shalt not consent unto him, nor hearken unto him, neither shall thine eye pity him, neither shalt thou spare him, neither shalt thou conceal him. But thou shalt surely kill him; thine hand shall be first upon him to put him to death, and afterward the hand of all the people. And thou shalt stone him with stones that he die."

This is the religious liberty of God; the toleration of Jehovah. If I had lived in Palestine at that time, and my wife, the mother of my children, had said to me, "I am tired of Jehovah, he is always asking for blood; he is never weary of killing; he is always telling of his might and strength; always telling what he has done for the Jews, always asking for sacrifices; for doves and lambs-blood, nothing but blood.—

Let us worship the sun.   Jehovah is too revengeful, too malignant, too exacting. Let us worship the sun. The sun has clothed the world in beauty; it has covered the earth with flowers; by its divine light I first saw your face, and my beautiful babe."—If I had obeyed the command of God, I would have killed her. My hand would have been first upon her, and after that the hands of all the people, and she would have been stoned with stones until she died. For my part, I would never kill my wife, even if commanded so to do by the real God of this universe. Think of taking up some ragged rock and hurling it against the white bosom filled with love for you; and when you saw oozing from the bruised lips of the death wound, the red current of her sweet life—think of looking up to heaven and receiving the congratulations of the infinite fiend whose commandment you had obeyed!

Can we believe that any such command was ever given by a merciful and intelligent God? Suppose, however, that God did give this law to the Jews, and did tell them that whenever a man preached a heresy, or proposed to worship any other God that they should kill him; and suppose that afterward this same God took upon himself flesh, and came to this very chosen people and taught a different religion, and that thereupon the Jews crucified him; I ask you, did he not reap exactly what he had sown? What right would this God have to complain of a crucifixion suffered in accordance with his own command? ...

If the Pentateuch be true, religious persecution is a duty. The dungeons of the Inquisition were temples, and the clank of every chain upon the limbs of heresy was music in the ear of God. If the Pentateuch was inspired, every heretic should be destroyed; and every man who advocates a fact inconsistent with the sacred book, should be consumed by sword and flame.

In the Old Testament no one is told to reason with a heretic, and not one word is said about relying upon argument, upon education, nor upon intellectual development—nothing except simple brute force. Is there today a Christian who will say that four thousand years ago, it was the duty of a husband to kill his wife if she differed with him upon the subject of religion? Is there one who will now say that, under such circumstances, the wife ought to have been killed? Why should God be so jealous of the wooden idols of the heathen? Could he not compete with Baal? Was he envious of the success of the Egyptian magicians? Was it not possible for him to make such a convincing display of his power as to silence forever the voice of unbelief? Did this God have to resort to force to make converts? Was he so ignorant of the structure of the human mind as to believe all honest doubt a crime? If he wished to do away with the idolatry of the Canaanites, why did he not appear to them? Why did he not give them the tables of the law? Why did he only make known his will to a few wandering savages in the desert of Sinai?

CONCLUSION

...

If the Pentateuch is inspired, the civilization of our day is a mistake and crime. There should be no political liberty. Heresy should be trodden out beneath the bigot's brutal feet. Husbands should divorce their wives at will, and make the mothers of their children houseless and weeping wanderers. Polygamy ought to be practiced; women should become slaves; we should buy the sons and daughters of the heathen and make them bondmen and bondwomen forever. We should sell our own flesh and blood, and have the right to kill our slaves. Men and women should be stoned to death for laboring on the seventh day. "Mediums," such as have familiar spirits, should be burned with fire. Every vestige of mental liberty should be destroyed, and reason's holy torch extinguished in the martyr's blood.

Is it not far better and wiser to say that the Pentateuch—while containing some good laws, some truths, some wise and useful things—is, after all, deformed and blackened by the savagery of its time? Is it not far better and wiser to take the good and throw the bad away?

CPSIA information can be obtained at www.ICGtesting.com
Printed in the USA
LVOW060716110113

315178LV00001B/155/A